Bonuses Include:

FREE access to my exclusive web-based Ultimate Property Analyzer software that will enable you to analyze any deal in two seconds flat! Includes a video tutorial to show you exactly how to use it!

FREE audio training and special report on how to buy real estate in your IRA or retirement account!

FREE training video of one of my Realtors making HUD offers for me—live!

FREE training video on how to buy and sell your HUD homes the same day (Real Estate Day Trading!)

FREE 7-part video series on how to sell your low-priced HUD homes for 3-6 times what you paid for them, earning 119% returns or more by using seller financing!

FREE 30-minute strategy session phone conversation with a team member in my office, who will answer all of your questions and help you get started making money on HUD homes right away! During this 30-minute session, we can help you determine the best way to get started investing in real estate—whether through HUD homes specifically or through any number of the methods I practice and teach!

FREE tickets for you and a guest to my Three Day Training Boot Camp event taught personally by my team and me. We hold 6-8 of these a year all over the USA!

FREE addition to my wholesale buyers' list to get first notification of my deeply discounted properties before other investors do, as well as a video presentation I have prepared for you.

FREE customized spreadsheet that I use to keep track of all of my HUD offers.

To access all of your bonuses please look for the website link and access code throughout this book.

HUD Homes Half Off!
A step-by-step, detailed guide to simplify the process for buying HUD homes at 50, 40, even 30% of value!

By Larry H. Goins
Copyright © 2012 Goins Group, LLC

ISBN-13: 978-1480094277
ISBN-10: 1480094277

Disclaimer

HUD HOMES HALF OFF!

A step-by-step,
detailed guide
to simplify the process
for buying HUD homes
at 50, 40, even 30% of
value!

By LARRY H. GOINS

DEDICATION
AND ACKNOWLEDGEMENTS

I want to thank my family that I love very much. My wife Pam, daughter Linda, son Noah, and my mom, Ann.

Thank you, Andy Laikin for all the wisdom and knowledge in real estate and business that you shared with me. You are the guru's guru. Thanks, Dad.

I would also like to thank all of my team members, who work hard every day running my real estate business, taking care of all of our students, and keeping our core values and mission statement alive and well.

Sharon Alverson, Nathan Amaral, Melanie Bell, Kandas Broome, Audrey Burlacu, Amanda Busby, Brenda Cavanaugh, Nicole Coleman, Gene Corbett, Kenny Culver, Randolph Cunningham, Mahdi Dean, Ronald Devine, Mike Feeney, Melissa Floyd, Ginis Garcia, Steve Gatewood, Diana Giel, John Hearn, Leon Humphrey, Tom Konapitsky, Mike McKenzie, Lorrie Morris, Liz Nechio, Gabriela Ojeda, Paul Olson, Ed Reckdenwald, Michael Sampson, Todd Sorensen, Diana Stephenson, Wendy Sweet, Dean West, and Lisa Williams.

TABLE OF CONTENTS

ABOUT THE AUTHOR
Larry is taking real estate investment training to the highest level!

Larry H. Goins has been licensed as a mortgage lender and mortgage broker in North Carolina and South Carolina. He has also been licensed in both North Carolina and South Carolina as a real estate broker and general contractor. He is a past member of the North Carolina Association of Mortgage Professionals and National Association of Mortgage Professionals. Larry has been investing in real estate for over 20 years.

In the past, Larry has served as President of the Metrolina Real Estate Investors Association in Charlotte, NC, a not-for-profit organization that has over 350 members and is the local chapter of the National Real Estate Investors Association.

Larry is an active real estate investor who travels the US speaking and training audiences at conventions, expos and Real Estate Investment Associations on his strategies for buying 10-15 properties per month without ever leaving his office. He has purchased properties in 10 different states from his office in Lake Wylie, South Carolina.

This is Larry's second book. His first book, *Getting Started in Real Estate Day Trading,* which teaches how to buy and sell houses the same day using the internet, is available wherever books are sold.

You can also get an autographed copy, which will include your name and a personal message from Larry at his website: **www.HUDHomesHalfOff.com.**

Between speaking engagements and mentoring other investors, Larry oversees the daily operations of his real estate investment company that buys and wholesales 10-15 or more properties per month to other investors at 70% or less of the ARV (after-repaired value). Larry also rehabs some properties to sell at retail to owner occupants and keeps some as rentals as well.

On a personal note, Larry and his wife, Pam, have two children, Linda and Noah. He is a member of New River Community Church in Lake Wylie, SC and occasionally plays guitar in the Church Praise Team. As a Husband, Father, Business Man and Real Estate Investor, Larry holds true to his core values and moral integrity. His personal and business motto is to ***"Put People and Principles Before Profits; When You Do That, Everyone Profits."***

INTRODUCTION

Hello, and welcome to the wonderful world of HUD homes. If you are reading this, you are either a real estate investor who wants to take advantage of the many properties that can be bought today at a discount, or a savvy homebuyer looking to get a good deal on your first or next personal residence.

I'm Larry Goins, a real estate investor and private money lender in South Carolina, and I teach people like yourself how to make money in real estate through proven, "out of the box" methods—even if you are starting out with no credit or cash to put down on properties.

I'm going to address real estate investors specifically in this book, as that is my background and probably includes the majority of people who are reading this book.

But if you are looking for a home to live in yourself (and investors need homes, too) then read this with your investor glasses on, because that same mindset will help you to find what you're looking for to live in and save a lot of money in the process. You may even decide that you would like to make some money investing in real estate by the time you finish reading this book.

I want to take just a minute to tell you about our Mission Statement and Core Values. When you start and run a business it is important that everyone on board know the philosophy of the business and the owners. You need to set the tone of your business and how it will be run. This will help you when you start bringing in others to help grow your business. If you have your own set of core values and a mission statement, you will be able to keep them in mind when hiring new people and working with customers. If you visit our office in Lake Wylie, SC, you will see these hanging in the lobby and in at least four other places throughout our offices—our Mission Statement and Core Values.

OUR MISSION STATEMENT

**To provide hope, encouragement and opportunity
to individuals and their families,
by providing quality products, services,
properties and mentoring,
based on ethical, moral and biblical principles.**

CORE VALUES WE LIVE BY

1. **We Put People And Principles Before Profits**
2. **We Expect, Embrace And Adapt To Change**
3. **We Are Adventurous, Creative, Open Minded And Have Fun**
4. **We Take Ownership, Are Accountable And Challenge Ourselves**
5. **We Are Good Stewards Of The Company's Money, Resources And Our Time**
6. **We Nurture Each Customer In Every Interaction To Create A Lifetime Raving Fan**
7. **We Keep A Sense Of Urgency, Positive Attitude And Do Our Best**

8. **We Are Committed To Personal Excellence And Self Improvement**
9. **We Build A Positive Team And Family Spirit**
10. **We Are Humble And Do The Right Thing**

Before starting your business, I hope you will create your own set of core values and a mission statement that reflects who you are and how you want to run your business and life.

Now Is The Time To Get Deals On Houses

If you have been paying attention to the news and real estate market in the last few years, you have probably noticed that with hard economic times has come a surge in loan defaults, foreclosures, short sales, and repossessed homes.

With these challenges comes this opportunity for those with the courage to think big and take action to follow through. Homes that have been foreclosed are typically sold for less than market value—sometimes far below. I have personally purchased HUD homes as low as 30% of the list price.

The banks and government institutions that now own these properties are not in the business of keeping real estate on their books for long. In fact, they want to get rid of them ASAP to improve their financial statements. So they are often willing to take the loss in order to recoup some of the money they originally spent.

You stand to profit by buying them at a discount, fixing them up, and reselling them again for a quick profit—which I call a "fix and flip."

Or, you may buy homes today at very depressed prices and hold onto them as part of a long-term, wealth-building strategy. Getting houses for a fraction of what they were once worth means the values have plenty of room to come up when the market corrects itself. In addition to the market conditions, we are purchasing properties at 30% to 50% less than the current asking or list price, which is even better.

In other words, you don't want to buy when the market is at its peak—so now is the time! You also don't want to pay list price, which will almost insure a profit for you assuming everything else with a property checks out. We will cover this later in the book.

Even in today's tougher market, my team and I buy and sell 10 to 15 or more deals per month—and most of our properties are sold the same day (although we do rehab some to retail and also keep some as rentals). No more rehabs, tenants or long-term financing; we are in and out of each property quickly.

Traditional Methods Of Finding Distressed Properties

Over the years, I have constantly tested and tried new ways of finding motivated sellers willing to sell their property far below market value. Some of it involves proactive marketing, such as mailing letters and postcards or running ads to get people to respond.

This can be time consuming and often requires an upfront investment in marketing costs, which a lot of beginning investors or aspiring homeowners don't have.

One alternative is to get a good real estate agent to help you find properties that might be a potential deal. I have done this many times with success and wholeheartedly recommend getting one or several buyers' agents to pound the pavement, searching for deals on your behalf.

But this can also be time consuming, as you may need to invest a few hours in each potential deal, researching its value, driving out to do a walk-through, and finding out the facts about the house piecemeal—it can be a real organizational mess.

Why I Wrote This Book

I decided to create this book in order to show my students a simpler method for finding deals that I believe every investor needs to try for the following reasons:

•The list of HUD homes for sale is readily available to anyone, even without a real estate license. This makes your job of finding suitable properties to look into easier in the first place. There is also a limited amount available each month—so it's usually manageable to stay on top of without being overwhelmed.

•The best part is that you don't have to gather the information you need about each property in bits and pieces in order to make an intelligent offer. HUD has the list organized pretty well in advance for you to use. Of course, you'll always need to do your own due diligence, but these numbers can be used as rough estimates to save time, and you can verify them later on.

•Another advantage of bidding on HUD properties is the bidding process is streamlined and simple. When the time comes, an agent will submit your offer online and you'll get an answer back the next day if it is accepted, or if they have made you a counter offer. Typically, it's either accepted or rejected, but if it is rejected they will not send any response at all. The offer simply expires and the property is still open to new bids for the current day.

•Since you are not dealing with homeowners and the emotional element that can comes with it, you bypass much of this to a degree any time you use an agent, but with HUD homes especially, you're dealing with an organization that has its own policies and procedures. This means that it gets efficient and predictable after a while.

•Remember, it's a numbers game. Each offer you make can be done in a relatively short amount of time, so if you are dedicated to making multiple offers each week, it's just a matter of time until one is accepted. It might take 25, 50, or even 100 offers or more to get one accepted at the low prices I will show you how to buy at. If you expect that going in, you will not get disappointed after making several offers without getting a positive response.

•Another advantage of working with HUD is that there is little competition. Most investors are chasing after people in foreclosure or trying to buy properties at auction. And when you submit your bid, HUD will only compare your offer to any other offers that happened to have been submitted that same day (if any) before making their decision. Typically, you don't have multiple people making offers on the same day. Now, depending on the market you live in, there could be competition. If you are an investor and live in an area where there is competition, I suggest making offers in a different market where there is not as much competition.

•With HUD you can get big discounts. I'm not saying this because I heard it somewhere; I'm saying it because I do deals all the time and can show you examples. So, if you find a local real estate agent who tries to tell you that HUD will not accept offers under 80% or 90%, don't bother listening.

Perhaps they have never seen someone actually do it, but you need people on your team who believe in the same possibilities you see or else they will not last long working with you. And remember, it is a numbers game, so whichever agent you find is going to have to put in some work.

One thing that I have found is that the lower the price of the property, the lower a bid they will accept. For example, I have purchased many houses that were listed for around $30,000 and ended up paying around $10,000, which is about 33% of list. It is much more difficult to get a 33% bid accepted on a house listed for $100,000.

SPECIAL BONUS

We have a strategy that allows us to capitalize on this by buying dirt-cheap houses that no one else wants. We then sell them for 3-6 times what we paid by selling them with seller financing. We have gotten returns from 119% to 788% on our investment by receiving monthly payments and getting paid more over time. This is a great concept that works extremely well in today's market. I call this my *Filthy Riches* strategy. If you would like to learn more about this, please visit **www.HUDHomesHalfOff.com** and enter access code HUD1 to get a FREE 7-part Video Series, register for a training webinar, and much more.

Larry Goins

.

CHAPTER ONE:
Real-Life Examples of Real Deals

Before I jump into explaining what HUD homes are and how the system works, I want to give you some real life examples of real deals that I've bought recently and resold quickly for a nice profit. I want you to see the kinds of properties that are available and the profit potential that you could be making once you prefect this strategy.

Below is the first example:

Example #1:

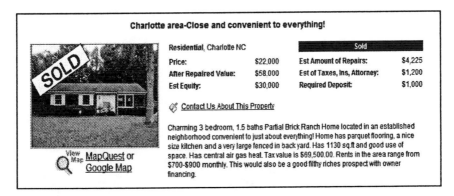

Charlotte area-Close and convenient to everything!

Residential, Charlotte NC		Sold	
Price:	$22,000	Est Amount of Repairs:	$4,225
After Repaired Value:	$58,000	Est of Taxes, Ins, Attorney:	$1,200
Est Equity:	$30,000	Required Deposit:	$1,000

Contact Us About This Property

Charming 3 bedroom, 1.5 baths Partial Brick Ranch Home located in an established neighborhood convenient to just about everything! Home has parquet flooring, a nice size kitchen and a very large fenced in back yard. Has 1130 sq.ft and good use of space. Has central air gas heat. Tax value is $69,500.00. Rents in the area range from $700-$900 monthly. This would also be a good filthy riches prospect with owner financing.

View Map MapQuest or Google Map

Here is a screen shot from my website **www.InvestorsRehab.com** *of a home that was listed on HUD's website at $30,000. The property description estimated that it needs $3,000-$5,000 of repairs, based on the contractor's estimate that HUD ordered. It just needs paint and carpet, nothing major.*

And our research showed that it could sell for $58,000 once the repairs were done and it looked nice again. What would you offer for the house? We made an offer of $10,250, which was accepted… so if anyone tells you how HUD will only agree to some minimal percentage of a property's value, don't believe it! They can—and will.

We resold this house to another investor for $22,000 and let him do all the fix up and take it from there. He is now renting it out for $675 per month and making a great cash flow for his efforts and has plenty of equity built in if he decides to sell for a profit.

From this one deal, we pocketed an easy $12,000 (minus closing costs) and moved on to the next one. As previously mentioned, the screenshot is from my website, where I posted all of the details to make it available to investor's on my buyers' list. This house was in North Carolina, which may have a different market value than many other areas of the country but it was a good deal for us and our buyer.

But note that house values do not have to be lower than the national average in order for you to make money with HUD homes; you just need to buy them at a large discount off of whatever each individual properties resale value will be (once fixed up) in your area. I'll cover this more in the section about making offers.

Following Is Another Example:

Example #2:

GREAT RENTAL OR OWNER FINANCING PROPERTY

Residential, High Point NC		Sold	
Price:	$23,000	Est Amount of Repairs:	$795
After Repaired Value:	$60,000	Est of Taxes, Ins, Attorney:	$1,900
Est Equity:	$34,000	Required Deposit:	$1,000

✆ Contact Us About This Property

MapQuest or Google Map

Nice solid ranch style home with 3 bedrooms/1 bath and 1047 sq.ft. Good location - close to High Point University, .53 miles, and shopping. Freshly painted interior with minimal repairs needed. Neighborhood is mostly owner occupied, but has been managed as a rental property for years. Would make a great rental or owner financing property.
Can be purchased with 1706 Gavin Drive in the same neighborhood for a discount!

This is another HUD home that we found recently with a tax assessor's value of $85,000. Now, it may be worth more or less than that, but the tax assessor's guide is often a close enough guide to go off when initially looking at a property—especially if, like this house, it started out being listed for $45,000. In the past, in most areas the tax value was usually lower than the actual value. We have found that now it is typically a little higher than actual value.

See the spread between the house's resale value and its listing price? This is a huge indicator that you should spend more time looking into this and possibly making an offer on it.

In fact, this house was originally listed for $45,000 and then the price dropped down to $35,000 and then later was further reduced to $30,000. We ended up buying it for $10,125 and currently have another investor to flip it to for $23,000.

This is called wholesaling deals—getting a good one under contract and then getting a cash buyer to take it off your hands for more than your negotiated price, but with plenty of profit left for my wholesale buyer to fix it up, flip it and make a nice profit.

In this case we will profit about $13,000, minus closing costs. We could also fix it up, and resell it or hold it as a rental property, but in this case we just plan on making a quick profit but leaving plenty of profit in the deal for our buyer.

As a follow up, at the time of this writing, we are still waiting for HUD to settle some title issues that it's responsible to clean up before the closing can proceed. Yes, sometimes even HUD has some title issues that have to be worked out before closing. But rest assured that when you close on a HUD home, you will be issued clear title to the property with no outstanding liens or judgments. You also need to always get title insurance when purchasing a property. This is something that is handled by the closing agent, which could be an attorney or title company, depending on the state the property is located in. I will talk more about that later.

These are good examples of the types of deals that I like and that you should be looking for. These are the types of low purchase prices that are possible.

We sometimes make 25, 50 or 100 offers or more to get a property at a very deep discount. We then put it on our website after performing all of our due diligence to make sure it is really a great deal. After we know it is a great investment, we then resell it for a little bit more—as you have seen here—to my VIP Buyers' List.

To get notified of screaming deals like these, simply go to **www.HUDHomesHalfOff.com** and enter access code HUD1 to get on my "VIP Buyers' List." I have also prepared a special video there for you.

Following Are Some More Examples Of Real HUD Home Deals

Example #3:

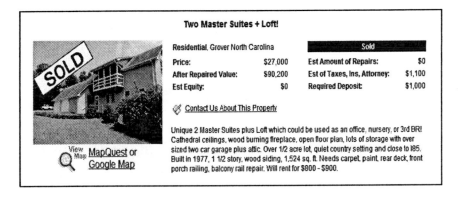

Two Master Suites + Loft!

Residential, Grover North Carolina

		Sold	
Price:	$27,000	Est Amount of Repairs:	$0
After Repaired Value:	$90,200	Est of Taxes, Ins, Attorney:	$1,100
Est Equity:	$0	Required Deposit:	$1,000

Contact Us About This Property

Unique 2 Master Suites plus Loft which could be used as an office, nursery, or 3rd BR! Cathedral ceilings, wood burning fireplace, open floor plan, lots of storage with over sized two car garage plus attic. Over 1/2 acre lot, quiet country setting and close to I85. Built in 1977, 1 1/2 story, wood siding, 1,524 sq. ft. Needs carpet, paint, rear deck, front porch railing, balcony rail repair. Will rent for $800 - $900.

View Map MapQuest or Google Map

This house was listed for sale for $45,000. Our research (more about research later) indicated it could resell for $90,000 after repairs. All it needed was carpet and a new deck in the back. We bid and bought it for $15,300. We resold it to another investor for $27,000.

Now here is something funny and interesting. The investor who purchased this property from us was actually a Realtor. He had seen the property listed on HUD's website for $45,000 but was able to purchase it from us for $27,000, which was still much less than he thought he could get it for.

By the way, as a side note, throughout this book I will be using the term *Realtor* sometimes and *real estate agent* sometimes as well. Just to clarify, a Realtor is a licensed real estate agent or broker who is a member of the National Association of Realtors. Most all real estate agents or brokers these days are members of the National Association of Realtors, which makes them a *Realtor*.

Okay, back to my Realtor buyer who bought the house. Our deals are so good that Realtors buy from us! Had he read my book, he could have just purchased it from HUD himself. But remember, there are plenty of deals to go around. Don't think that because many people are reading my book that all of the deals will disappear. The sad fact is that most people who read a book or invest in education never do anything with it. Please don't let that be you. I want you to be successful, and I will do everything I can to help you!

You've probably noticed that there's a lot of money to be made wholesaling deals to other investor buyers. I like this strategy of wholesaling so much that I have a team of full-time investors in my office who make offers all day long on HUD houses and other bank owned properties.

So as you can see, there is a wealth of opportunity out there for you with HUD homes. You don't have to use your own money, and you don't have to have credit or be able to qualify for a loan. I will show you later how to get the money. You don't have to drive out to see a lot of properties or engage in fierce bidding wars with other people.

Just keep in mind that *you will have to make multiple offers before one is accepted*. When the first few are turned down, don't get discouraged or let someone tell you that these low offers will never be accepted.

What if you find out that other bidders are going to see the house or have made offers on the same day as you? My suggestion is to go about your business like you normally would—submit your bid and name your price like we'll show you, then let the chips fall where they may. Don't let the fact that someone else is interested discourage you! Take my word for it… some will, some won't. It's truly a numbers game.

For more information on how I run my wholesale operation, visit **www.HUDHomesHalfOff.com** and enter access code HUD1.

Here, you can sign up for a FREE 10-part eCourse, register for an upcoming training webinar that details the process, and much more.

Example #4:

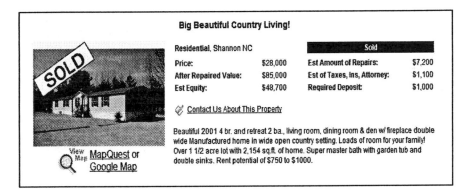

This one was a four-bedroom doublewide listed for a little under $50,000. It didn't need significant repairs at all. It was in good shape. We bought it for around $15,000.

Note that you can still get good deals on HUD homes needing little or no repairs. Some people keep their property in great condition but, unfortunately, lose it due to financial problems. But generally, the more repairs needed, the more likely your low offer will be accepted.

This one provided another quick and tidy profit for us through wholesaling—a fantastic opportunity for beginners or those wanting to bypass managing repairs or tenants. Wholesaling is one of the fastest ways to generate some immediate cash as a new investor.

I bought this property in my Self Directed Roth IRA, where the profits will be tax-deferred for life. Imagine that...did you know you can use your IRA or retirement account to invest in real estate?

Example #5:

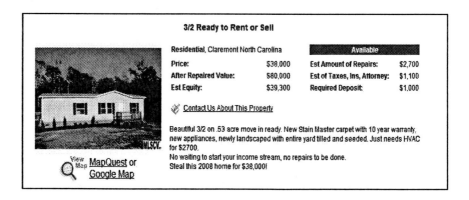

This home was listed for $50,000 on the HUD website. There were two other houses on the same street that were listed for $85,000 and $69,900. It needed about $6,000 in repairs— including carpeting, a stove and fridge, and a new HVAC unit in the back. We put it on our website as a wholesale deal "as is" but later decided to retail it.

We bought it for $18,000 and decided to retail it as mentioned above. We put about $6,000 in repairs into it, then listed it with a local Realtor and sold it within 90 days for $54,000 to a person who is going to live in. We made $30,000 on this little mobile home in about 90 days. Is that great or what? You can do the same thing!

Just because my examples are low-priced properties, I don't want you to think that I only buy cheap properties. I do buy a lot of cheap properties, but I have also purchased many more expensive properties. We have bought many houses for $50,000–$100,000; however, as previously mentioned, it is more difficult to get HUD to accept a much lower offer on the more expensive properties. But on the plus side, the more expensive properties are usually easier to retail (although there are fewer buyers that can qualify for more expensive properties) and have more profit built into them if you will follow my formula, as I will outline a little later.

Larry Goins

CHAPTER TWO:
What Exactly Are HUD Homes?

The government entity I'm referring to as HUD stands for the Department of Housing and Urban Development.

FHA loans have been helping people become homeowners since 1934. How do they do it? The Federal Housing Administration (FHA)—which is part of HUD—insures the loan, so your lender can offer you a better deal such as:

- •Low down payments
- •Low closing costs
- •Easier credit qualifying

When a lender makes an FHA loan it is basically being insured by HUD. What this means is that a bank or mortgage company (not HUD) is lending money to a homeowner to purchase a home. The borrower pays the money back to the bank in monthly payments and hopefully, doesn't fall behind.

If the homeowner does fall behind, rather than foreclosing on the property themselves like most mortgage companies would do, the bank will file a claim on the insurance policy they have, since HUD insured the loan. Then once the bank has been paid for the loan they made, they hand it over to HUD to foreclose (repossess) and try to resell again on their website through a Realtor that is approved to list HUD homes (**www.HUDHomeStore.com**). From that point, the bank doesn't have to deal with getting the house off of its books.

The property then becomes what we call a HUD home as opposed to a regular bank REO, or foreclosed home. These homes are made available for sale on HUD's website through certain agents who have been approved by HUD.

HUD will hire an asset manager who will manage the securing and disposition of the property. This will include having a contractor or manager do a walk-through of the property and list the repairs needed and estimate what it will cost to take care of them.

They also winterize the house to make sure that no pipes burst during cold weather and secure it with locked doors and boarded windows, if needed. But they don't do any repairs to it prior to listing it for sale. They don't want to spend the extra money to do so. HUD has done some repairs in the past, but as of right now I do not know of any properties that they are making the needed repairs on before listing them for sale. This is why there are such great opportunities for you to buy at low prices—because you are among a small group of people willing to take on a house needing repairs. And the more repairs it needs, the fewer people there are willing to buy it. So keep this in mind when you are scanning for deals to bid on. Also, I think it is important to note that some of the properties HUD sells do not need much work at all, as we have seen from my examples.

Who Can Purchase HUD Properties?

Anyone can purchase HUD properties—including you! This is not some game that only the good ol' boys in your town or those with tons of capital are able to play. As you'll see in future chapters of this book, there are ways to come up with the financing yourself even if you don't have cash or credit of your own.

But there are time constraints that you have to work within. As an investor, you can't bid on HUD homes until they have been on the market at least thirty days. Prior to that, only owner-occupants and nonprofit entities are able to bid. Owner occupants take precedence over nonprofits and government agencies.

When the time comes, you will need to select a real estate agent who is already registered to bid on HUD homes to make your offers—which, as you'll see, is easy enough for the Realtor to get set up to do. You could even contact the listing agent if you want to have them make the offer for you. Just click on the "Agent Info" tab when looking at a property on HUD's website to get the agent's contact information (**www.HUDHomeStore.com**).

In the next section, we're going to dive into the details of how to scan for HUD homes online, get the information you need, and submit an offer like the ones we make every day. Hold onto your seats because this is where it gets really exciting!

Larry Goins

Visit **www.HUDHomesHalfOff.com** to claim your bonuses

CHAPTER THREE:
Finding Deals

Your search for available HUD homes will begin at the website HUD has set up for this purpose: **www.HUDHomeStore.com.**

You or your agent can also find HUD homes listed on the Multiple Listing Service (MLS), but since they are all listed at this website, it's easier for you or your agent to just go there. You could scan for new HUD listings on a weekly or daily basis before choosing which to bring to your agent's attention or investigate further.

Or, if you have an agent search these for you regularly, make sure to be very clear with them what to bring to you; otherwise, they may bring you many properties to sift through that doesn't meet your criteria, and you won't end up saving any time.

As a wholesaler and investor, I sometimes keep some homes as rentals, and I also fix some of the properties up to retail to owner-occupied buyers. I like to look for houses that have at least three bedrooms and some curb appeal. I also do not make offers on anything less than 900 square feet. This is my basic buying criteria.

Let's go to **www.HUDHomeStore.com** now and take a look....

Here at HUD's website, you can see a "Search Properties" form right in the middle of the home page. This is where you can search for available properties according to your criteria.

HUD's property website is also a great source of other valuable information. The "HUD News" page has links to HUD's mission and history.

Press releases that HUD sends out are archived here, as well. This is where you can find out about updates and changes in their programs and terms that will help you understand the process better, or may give you a competitive advantage if you add what you learn here to your bidding process as an investor.

The HUD website has all kinds of resources available—check it out and look around. It's pretty self-explanatory. But make sure to check out:

- The lists of approved appraisers
- Fair market rents for different geographical areas
- FHA mortgage limits (useful to know when reselling a property)
- HUD forms and handbooks
- Loan calculators
- Lender locators
- Other useful tools for real estate investors.

If you would prefer to talk with a HUD agent first before starting your search, use the "Find a Broker" section to get the contact information of those in your city or zip code. They can help you to refine what you're looking for even further as an investor or home buyer.

For example, if the values of condos and townhomes in your area are depreciating in value or not rising at the same rate as other property types, or if your goal is to wholesale to other investors, then you may want to exclude them from your search or make lower offers on them than on the single family homes.

Beginning Your Search

In the "Search Properties" section on the home page, fill in the location, buyer type, type of properties you're looking for and status.

Start With Geography

Pick the state and county where you want to buy homes. If you are open to buying in several counties you will have to perform the search several times. I wouldn't fill in the city field if you are interested in all parts of one county.

You could leave the price range blank if you want to see every property in the specific area that is available. If you do select a price range, as an investor, the ideal price range is from right in the middle of the market to about halfway between the middle and the bottom—the bottom being the lowest-priced homes available. This is where you can be more certain homes can sell again because the loans are easier to qualify for (because of lower loan amounts). It is also a fact that the higher the price of the property, fewer people will be able to qualify for a loan.

For example, if the median price range in your area is $150,000, then you would be interested in properties from half of the median value (in this case $75,000) up to at or around the median price range of $150,000.

It's also interesting to scan the very bottom of price ranges and see what's happening there. You can find rare gems in properties that need some repairs, which can be opportunities for you.

You will generally want to have three bedrooms or more, and two full bathrooms or more, to be comfortable that you have an advantage when selling retail. In a tough market, you don't want to give buyers a reason not to buy your house, such as that it only has two bedrooms when they really want three, or only has one bathroom when they want two.

Then again, in your area you might sell two bedroom homes or homes with one bathroom just fine. This is where networking and knowing the market in your area will come in handy.

My team and I actually look at just about everything to a certain extent just to see what is available in the market and to get a feel for the number of properties available at certain price ranges. Remember, if you get a good enough deal on a property you can sell just about anything. I have sold houses with two bedrooms and one bath just fine—but we bought them at a steal.

Buyer Types

There are a few different buyer types on the HUD website to choose from. If you are buying as an investor, you'll need to choose "Investor" from among the options available. Below is a list of all of the options, with a brief description.

- **Owner-Occupant**—Those people who plan to buy a HUD home in order to live in it are often the only people who can bid on HUD homes in the first thirty days that they are on the market.

- **Investor**—After a home has been on the market for thirty days, the bidding is also opened up to people like you and me who want to buy these for a profit.

- **Good Neighbor Next Door**—Police officers, School Teachers, Firefighters, and Emergency Medical Technicians get a 50% incentive from the list price of the home. In turn, the buyer must commit to living in the home for 36 months, with that house as the sole residence.

- **Government Agency**—Some government agencies buy properties, and HUD gives them a chance to bid in advance of investors.

•**Nonprofit**—Nonprofit entities are also allowed to bid on homes less than thirty days on the market. How does this apply to you?

Several innovative investors in various parts of the country have formed nonprofit entities (as opposed to C or S corporations, LLC's, or some other entity to manage their investments and cash flow) in order to bid early, work out community financing or tax breaks, and other special privileges afforded to them.

Always consult an attorney when forming any entity, especially for the first time. And with a nonprofit you will want to find out special requirements and guidelines. Often, it needs to serve some community purpose, and if you specialize in buying houses dirt cheap and selling them to people or families with low income, you can create a special niche for yourself.

Some nonprofits are set up to buy and renovate homes with funds provided by donors or private lenders, and then sell the houses with built-in financing and collect money payments from the buyers, making more money in the long haul. Habitat for Humanity does this by building new homes using donations and volunteers.

You might also specialize in Section 8 rental housing, renting to seniors, or other ways of helping low income people as defined by HUD. And of course, as a nonprofit you can bid on properties before other investors during the first thirty days on the market.

By having almost exclusive access to bid on every new house before other investors, you can jump on the best deals first—the ones that other homeowners are shying away from.

So while you don't need to form a nonprofit to make money with HUD homes, hopefully this shows you that if you're creative while complying with the law, you can help people and help yourself at the same time.

Just make sure that if you go to the trouble to form a nonprofit that you are actually running a nonprofit. Remember to always do good, clean, business based on ethical and moral principles. I have actually done a lot of research on this and am in the process of forming a nonprofit myself to help low income people become homeowners.

$1 HUD Homes

HUD's Dollar Homes initiative helps local governments to foster housing opportunities for low to moderate income families and address specific community needs by offering them the opportunity to purchase qualified HUD-owned homes for $1 each. Generally, these properties are located in designated Revitalization Areas.

Dollar Homes are single-family homes that are acquired by the Federal Housing Administration (which is part of HUD) as a result of foreclosure actions. Single-family properties are made available through the program whenever FHA is unable to sell the homes for six months. Needless to say, these are also the homes that HUD has had a hard time selling.

By selling vacant homes for $1 after six months on the market, HUD makes it possible for communities to fix up the homes and put them to good use at a considerable savings. The newly occupied homes can then act as catalysts for neighborhood revitalization, attracting new residents and businesses to an area.

Local governments can partner with local nonprofit home-ownership organizations or tap into existing local programs to resell the homes to low- and moderate-income residents of the community.

HUD properties that have been offered for sale for one-hundred-and-eighty (180) days and that are not under a sales contract will be offered for purchase to local government agencies for a sales price of $1, along with applicable closing costs.

Can I Buy Multi-Family Properties From HUD?

While most of the properties HUD has for sale are single-family houses, it also insures mortgage on mutli-family properties—some of which fall behind and are repossessed along with apartments, nursing homes, hospitals, mobile home parks, and vacant land.

You won't find them listed with the houses though. At the time of this writing, you can subscribe to HUD's Multifamily Property Disposition Mailing List to be notified as new properties become available by going to **www.HUD.gov**, then selecting Program Offices, then Housing, then Multi-Family. Then, you can obtain the Free Info and Bid Kit from HUD for each property you're interested in.

Which Houses To Search For And Make Offers On

You might choose to make offers on every HUD home that meets certain criteria…so what are yours?

You could tell an agent to make an offer on everything that is under a certain price (such as the median price range in your area) following your formula for making offers and plugging in their best guess of the properties "as-is" value and repair estimate.

For the most part, you'll narrow down your search to the ones with the right number of bedrooms, bathrooms, square feet, desirable geographical areas, and have been on the market thirty days or more.

Don't worry about it if the house needs a lot of repairs. Those costs don't necessarily hit your wallet if you play your cards right. You can always wholesale it to another investor who can handle the improvements and big rehabs with no problems. More about that in a later chapter.

There is a term called "sweat equity," which refers to labor costs on fixing up a home. With any home you buy into, a little extra work on your part may be a great way to build some equity by doing some of the work yourself, but it depends on how much your time is worth to you.

From here, you can make offers on all of them that you want to, or just the ones showing additional signs of motivation (like price reductions, having a lot of repairs, long number of days on the market, etc.). Or, you could just focus on the best deals first and then get around to the rest later, if you have time. It's up to you!

Choosing The Status

You can choose to look at properties with any of the following statuses, but I just look at everything and go from there. Below is a listing of each status with a short description:

•**Accepting bids**—Generally where most homes are categorized.

•**New listing**—These are the homes that have just come on the market. You can't bid on these as an investor for thirty days.

•**Price reduced**—These are homes that have gone down in price since they were first listed.

•**Pending bid opening**—This is when a bid has been placed on a home, but the bid has not yet been accepted.

•**Showcase**—These homes do not need any renovation and are advertised as ready to move into. Remember, check each one out yourself or have someone check it out for you.

After choosing all the selections, click on the "search" button and you'll see a screen with the results, like the one on the following page.

Search Results for HUD Homes in Dallas, TX

Property Case	Address	Price	Status	Bed	Bath	Listing Period	Bid Open Date	Details
491-779909	6109 Symphony Ln Dallas, TX 75227 Dallas County	$81,000	⬇	3	2.00	Extended	01/21/2012	View Street Map it Email Info · Save
491-783711	6520 Oleta Drive Dallas, TX 75217 Dallas County	$47,700	⬇	4	3.00	Extended	01/21/2012	View Street Map it Email Info · Save
491-854910	1339 Trewitt Road Dallas, TX 75217 Dallas County	$43,843		4	2.00	Extended	01/21/2012	View Street Map it Email Info · Save
491-889139	9120 Sweetwater Drive Dallas, TX 75228 Dallas County	$140,000		3	2.00	Extended	01/21/2012	View Street Map it Email Info · Save
491-905212	2117 Autumn Meadow Trail Dallas, TX 75232 Dallas County	$74,800		3	2.00	Extended	01/21/2012	View Street Map it Email Info · Save
492-851381	513 Addison St Lake Dallas, TX 75065 Denton County	$108,000		3	2.00	Extended	01/21/2012	View Street Map it Email Info · Save

As you are learning in this chapter, the better you are at scanning, the fewer properties you will need to investigate further—unless your plan is to make an offer on everything. This is often the case if you live in a rural area or where there are not a lot of new HUD homes each month.

In small towns and rural markets, you can also try expanding your geographical search area. Perhaps there is a larger market or city an hour or two away from you. You can still find deals there and can wholesale them to other investors without having to drive there and look at every property.

Most of the investors who buy properties from me do not live in the same state, much less the same city. So don't think that just because you may not have any investor buyers in an area that you can't sell the property. With the age of the internet, many buyers purchase properties that they will never see.

On the search results page, you can also find out some additional key factors about the homes. You will also want to organize your search results to make it easier to analyze.

The first thing I do, if there are a lot of properties in the search results, is to put as many results on one page as you can. This keeps you from having to look at many pages to see all the properties in the search results.

You can also sort by Case Number. This is useful if you are tracking several offers on properties and want to just refer to them by their case number instead of writing their address every time. HUD tracks every property by case number. Write this down somewhere and you can refer to it later. I suggest in a spreadsheet where you can capture the same information for each property—such as property case number and price, number of bedrooms, number of bathrooms, list price, offer amount, date of offer, etc.

SPECIAL BONUS

As a bonus for purchasing this book, I have included my own personal spreadsheet that we use to organize the properties we want to make offers on. This is a great tool for keeping up with all of the properties, especially when you are making as many offers as we are. To get your own copy of the spreadsheet simply go to **www.HUDHomesHalfOff.com** and enter access code HUD1.

Next, sort the results by price. I usually go from high to low, but you could also sort with the lowest-priced homes first.

If you see a green arrow pointing downward it indicates that the price has been reduced. So if you can only make so many offers this week, I would target these first, as they have shown some kind of indicator that they are more eager to dispose of this property than the others. It shows that they are willing to negotiate.

Some will be marked with a pending sale graphic icon. You can keep an eye on these, but don't spend a lot of time looking into them further unless the buyer(s) doesn't end up purchasing and they come back on the market again.

Seeing pending sales are rare though, because they usually just take it off the website once an offer is accepted and HUD has received the contract from the buyer through their Realtor.

Larry Goins

CHAPTER FOUR:
Screening Deals

Getting The Property's Details

When you click on a property for sale, you'll be taken to its Property Details page, like this:

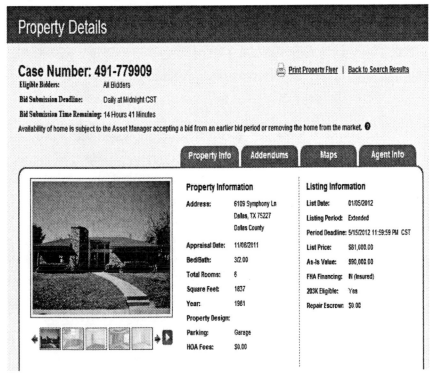

On this page you will be able to find everything you need to make your offer on the property. At the top is the property details, which lists the case number, the bidder type the property is available for, the bid deadline and time left to submit a bid that specific day.

On this page you will also find the picture of the property, and typically, there will be multiple pictures as well which helps you to get a feel of the condition of the property.

There are also several tabs on this page, and each one has a lot of information. The first, and default tab, that comes up when clicking on a specific property from the search results is the "Property Info" tab. Below is a detailed description of some of the items you will find on this page:

●**What's the "As-Is" Value?** This gives you the listing agent (or appraiser's) idea of what the house is currently worth. The first thing I do is compare the difference between the as-is value and the list price.

●**What is the list price?** Is it close to the as-is value, or is it already far below it? See if the price has been reduced already (or not) since it has been on the market, or if they started out low.

●**How many days has it been listed?** Is it now available for investors to bid on? Has the listing period been extended? Keep in mind that although you can begin to bid at thirty days, some people wait and only bid on properties sixty days or older.

The biggest price discounts typically happen around ninety days, as HUD's strategy is to continue dropping the prices until they are eventually sold.

•**What is the repair escrow?** The repair escrow is the estimate made by the field service manager on what it would cost to get the house in decent shape again.

Typically, there will be a Property Condition Report (PCR) attached in the Addendums section where you can look further into the details of the repairs needed.

Scroll through all the pictures of the property available. Try to get a feel for its curb appeal. Does it look good from the outside? There may be little things you will need to do that aren't listed in the PCR.

Is it eligible for FHA financing or 203k loan? These are important questions if you plan on getting those types of financing yourself—if you will be purchasing a HUD property to live in. Keep in mind, too, that after fixing it up, some buyers you will be selling to may want or need to get an FHA loan.

Addendums

In the Addendums tab you will find other disclosures and attachments that you will need to know before making your offer, or to include while submitting it.

These are helpful for double-checking that you have signed everything correctly. If there are any changes to the forms and what they mean, you will hear about it here first.

There is even a sample Investors Package you can look at. It shows how to fill in all the paperwork that you will need to take care of in the event your bid is successful.

Estimating Repairs

Check out the Property Condition Report (PCR) and note each of the line items on it. Look for items that are not functional and will have to be repaired or replaced:

Property Condition Report			
Case Number: 491-779909		Contract Area: 1D	
Current Step: 1c-Ready to Show Condition		Address: 6109 SYMPHONY LN	
Step Date: 11/03/2011		City, St Zip: DALLAS, TX 75227-0000	
HOC: Denver			

Property Condition Report		
Item Description/Condition	**Item Functionality**	**Functionality/Test Notes**
Cooling/Air-Conditioner: OK --Heating/Furnace: OK --HVAC System Duct: OK	HVAC tested and functional?: Yes	The furnace electronics were operational when the controls were activated, but there was no gas to test the burners. The A/C was in satisfactory condition. Gas was inactive at the time of inspection.
Electrical Wiring: OK --Other: N/A --Other: N/A	Electric supply tested and functional?: Yes	The electrical system was tested with an air compressor and there were no leaks detected. Electricity was inactive at the time of inspection.
Stove/Range/Oven: OK --Kitchen Cabinets: OK --Other: N/A	Built-in appliances tested and functional?: Yes	The appliances in place were in satisfactory condition at the time of inspection.
Plumbing: OK --Sink: OK --Other: N/A	Water supply tested and functional?: Yes	Pressure was applied using an air compressor and there were no leaks detected. Water was inactive at the time of inspection.
Water Heater: OK	Water heater functional?: Yes	There were no noted deficiencies at the time of inspection.
Sewer/Septic System: OK --Toilet: OK --Other: N/A	Sanitary & plumbing system functional?: Yes	There were no noted deficiencies at the time of inspection.
Roof: OK --Other: N/A	Roofing in acceptable condition?: Yes	There were no noted deficiencies with the roof at the time of inspection.

Do the same for missing items—if a sink is missing, it will be noted here. It gets pretty detailed.

Also, refer to the photos to get a feel for other things the house might need, like paint and carpet. These are often not mentioned in the PCR, but are items that will need to be done to please potential buyers or tenants down the road.

Your exit strategy will guide you when estimating repairs to make, too. For example, you might be able to get away with shampooing a carpet that has a few spots here and there if you plan to rent the house to tenants instead of fixing it up and retailing it to a new homeowner.

Today's qualified retail buyers are fewer, so if you plan on selling the house to someone who is going to live in it, you will probably need to go with fresh paint and new carpet—something neutral for the walls and floor, and white semi-gloss or gloss for the indoor trim. I just plan on having to paint every house we buy.

The photos will also alert you to things like a yard that needs attention. With the photos and the repair estimate available to you online, there isn't a lot of need to go see the house in person. If you did, it would be to confirm what you have already determined from all of the details on the website.

In other words, save your time and gas money. Make a tentative offer based on what you can ascertain about a home online. You'll have two business days after it is accepted to go see it or have someone else go see it and confirm your numbers before your contract and deposit has to get to the local HUD office.

Maps Section

Viewing the property in Google Maps is also helpful to get a feel for how far a drive it is from you and what kind of neighborhood it's in.

Homes in neighborhoods typically sell faster than more rural homes, but don't let that stop you. Just factor in the rural house taking a few months longer to sell if you will be fixing it up to retail to an owner occupant.

Maps and Directions

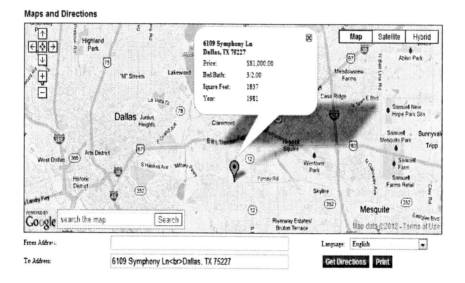

You can also see what part of town it's in. Is it in a war zone with homes that are falling apart? Is it in a high-crime area? What schools are nearby, and could they be a selling point?

Agent Info

In the Agent Info tab, you will find contact information for the various parties responsible for this home, as shown in the screen shot on the following page.

HUD Homes Half Off!

The Asset Manager is the HUD contractor responsible for the sale of the property. They are the ones who will receive the bid and accept or reject it, although the extent of their actual involvement in this—as opposed to a computer accepting or rejecting offers automatically—is up for debate. My guess is they don't get a lot of say in it, but rather than trying to figure out how they do what they do, I say make an offer that works for you and see what happens.

The Field Service Manager is responsible for maintaining the property. He takes care of the day-to-day maintenance, such as making sure the lawn is mowed, winterizing and un-winterizing, taking care of the carpet (sometimes, but not often), keeping the power on, etc.

The Listing Agent was hired by the asset manager to assist with the marketing of the home. You can make offers through them if you like. Just contact them using the phone number and email address they provide. They will simply submit your offer online at **www.HUDHomeStore.com.**

Digging Deeper

If you have done all of the following and feel like this property is going to be a good candidate for investment (or flipping), the next step is to dig deeper into getting details about the house.

If you can find out with a high assurance the things you need to know from just the Property Details page (the most important being time on market, price history, and repair estimates) then that is ideal.

Good Signs of a Potential Deal:

- **Needs Repairs**—The more, the better!

- **Price lowered**—The lower, the better!

- **Days on market**—The longer, the better!

But if you aren't sure, I suggest copying and pasting the property address into a Google search bar and see what comes up. Sometimes you will find the property listed on other websites, and these webpages will occasionally have more information about it than you could get from HUD's site.

Look for search results on these sites, as they will have a lot of information about the property:

www.Realtor

www.Zillow.com

www.Hotpads.com

www.Trulia.com

They will be the ones that come up near the top of the search results anyway.

About 11,700 results (0.27 seconds)

6109 Symphony Lane, Dallas TX | MLS# 11686466 - Trulia
www.trulia.com/.../3069606970-6109-Symphony-Ln-Dallas-TX-752...
Public Records for **6109 Symphony Ln**. Official property ... Price Comparison of **6109 Symphony Ln**. This Home ... Location Information near **6109 Symphony Ln** ...

6109 Symphony Ln, Dallas, TX 75227 | MLS# 11686466
www.redfin.com/TX/Dallas/6109-Symphony-Ln-75227/.../3090695...
For Sale: 3 bed, 2 bath, 1837 sq. ft. house located at **6109 Symphony Ln**, Dallas, TX 75227 on sale for $81000. MLS# 11686466. A fantastic buy. This well ...

6109 Symphony Ln Dallas TX 75227 - Public Property Records ...
www.realtor.com/.../6109-Symphony-Ln_Dallas_TX_75227_8b936...
If you want to acquire invaluable information about the property in Dallas, TX, ensure to look at **6109 Symphony Ln** Dallas TX 75227 property records.

6109 Symphony Ln Dallas TX - Home For Sale and Real Estate ...
www.realtor.com/.../6109-Symphony-Ln_Dallas_TX_75227_M7324...
Nov 16, 2011 – Details for **6109 Symphony Ln** Dallas TX. This property is for sale. Find out all the details on this property from Realtor.com.

6109 Symphony Ln, Dallas, TX 75227 MLS# 11686466 - Zillow
www.zillow.com › Texas › Dallas › Urbandale/Parkdale real estate
View 8 photos, tax records, sales history, and home values for **6109 Symphony Ln**. This home is listed for sale at $90000. A fantastic buy. This well maintained ...

Sometimes these sites will have more photos of the house that aren't found elsewhere. This might affect your repair estimation. For example, HUD may have pulled the old stinky carpet out of the house already, but did not replace it with new carpet.

If this is the case, then your carpet replacement costs will not be as high. See what I mean? Always try to get a better view of the houses' interiors.

You might not have noticed this unless you saw more recent photos posted on a different website. You can also find comps that previous agents have pulled of similar, nearby houses that have recently sold. The same goes for similar listings of current properties. These can help you estimate the current market value.

And, sometimes you'll see that the home was listed previously at a higher price, which can clue you in that the price is now reduced (which is sometimes not reflected on HUD's site).

What If I Can't Find Anything?

If your Google search does not come up with any helpful websites like the above, try it again, but this time take out some of the information, like the word "Drive" or "Dr."

You can also put quotations around the property address, such as "123 Magnolia Drive" to only find results showing those three words in that exact order.

Or, try removing the "City, State" from the property address, as there is a LOT of stuff online with cities and states mentioned.

So if you exclude them, you'll get fewer results, but hopefully, you'll get more of exactly what you're looking for. If you do a search without listing the city or state, make sure you are looking at the correct property when looking at your search results pages.

Larry Goins

.

CHAPTER FIVE:
Making Offers To Buy

When you have found a house that you're ready to make an offer on and you have your financing in place, the next step is to have your Realtor or the listing agent submit your bid online at **www.HUDHomeStore.com.**

To submit an offer, you will need to be a HUD-registered Selling Broker; otherwise, submit your offer through somcone who is. HUD only accepts offers made through real estate agents that have applied for and received an NAID number from HUD, and who are registered as a Bidder at www.HUDHomeStore.com.

Special Bonus

I know that coming up with offers and making them in real life has been a high-stress activity for a lot of investors. To help you get more comfortable with taking action on this part of the book, I have a behind-the-scenes video of actual offers being made on HUD's website waiting for you. Watch, as one of my Realtors makes an offer live in this exclusive video recording of her computer screen as she explains the entire process. It's one of the FREE bonuses you get for owning this book. To claim yours, visit **www.HUDHomesHalfOff.com**, and enter access code "HUD1."

Here's the page...

Getting A NAID Number

Pretty much any real estate broker can get one of these by sending HUD an NAID application package along with the required forms and documents to the HUD Homeownership Center that has jurisdiction over the state where they're located.

There is a page on HUD's site called "NAID Application" where you can apply for a NAID number if you are a Selling Broker, Nonprofit, or Government Agency.

What About Associate Brokers And Sales Agents?

Once the Principal Broker has registered, agents can register to use **www.HUDHomeStore.com** using their Principal Broker's NAID number and their own real estate license number and begin to submit bids.

Finding A Broker To Make Offers

If you need to find a registered Agent or Broker to make offers for you, the listing agent's name and the property information is listed in the Agent Info section at **www.HUDHomeStore.com**. Contact the listing agent using the phone and email address provided and ask them to make the offer for you. Alternatively, you can look at the "Find a Broker" page shown here, where you can search for an agent to work with by name, city, state, or zip code.

Selling Brokers Must Provide The Following:

- Form 1111—Send the original and one copy of the 1111 Form

- Form 1111A

- IRS Letter 147 C or IRS Official Document reflecting your Business Name and EIN, or copy of social security card if operating under your social security number

- Copy of your Real Estate Broker's License with Expiration Date

- Copy of your Driver's License with Expiration Date

- Recent Utility Bill or Bank Statement that supports the address and Company or Broker name shown on Form 1111

Should I Use An Agent?

If you're already a real estate agent, it probably isn't a big deal to register and get your own NAID number in a short period of time.

But if you're not an agent, then personally, I think it's a lot easier to just make offers through a registered HUD agent, especially at first if you are just trying out the HUD home game for yourself.

You might commit to an initial goal of making 50-100 offers through other agents and seeing how it goes before jumping in and getting your real estate license—if you want to go that far. Or, you might do a few deals first before deciding it's worth it to be able to submit them yourself and have access to market data and sales prices, etc. I have been licensed for years, but I do not keep my license current, and I always go through another licensed agent. Yes, I know I could also get the commission if I did it myself, but I would rather have another agent working for me, submitting my offers and working to get me properties.

It's your choice; although I always emphasize making offers first and perfecting things later! But remember, when you're dealing with a real estate agent, they typically work and are paid by commission. They don't have time to waste, and neither do you.

So always respond quickly, make decisions quickly, and don't ask for more of their time than should be needed if you are not ready to take action on what they find out for you.

How Much Should I Offer?

One of the things that I have learned is that the lower the price of the property the lower percentage of list price they will accept. I have gotten offers accepted typically between 25% and 60% with most being in the 30% to 50% range.

Typically, the offers I make that are accepted have been around 30 to 40% of the listing price on lower priced homes and around 40 to 50% on higher priced homes. For example, if a house is listed for $30,000, then it is not unusual for me to get an offer of $10,000 accepted; however, if a house is listed for $100,000, they will probably not take $30,000 for it. Now they are both around 30% offers, but the higher the price, the less likely they are to take a 30% offer. On that $100,000 they would probably not take less than $50,000 to $60,000, based on my experience. Now don't think that every $100,000 house you make an offer on they will accept a 50 to 60% offer. It's not going to happen. Remember that we have to make lots of offers to get one accepted.

Some investors simply make an offer on every home that is available to them for some fixed percentage of market value, like 30 to 50% in my case.

The lower your offer is, the fewer will get accepted, but the more likely it is that when one is accepted it will be a screaming deal (and therefore a safer deal, especially if it is your first one).

We recently got a bid accepted of $28,000 on a house that was listed for $109,000. Now the reason we got this bid accepted was because the property was a two bedroom property; however, the property has almost 2000 square feet. So our thoughts were to simply figure in our repair estimate to add another bedroom within the existing square footage. There was plenty square footage to work with. So we made the offer and got it accepted.

This property had been on the market for almost 90 days so we knew HUD was ready to move it. After we got the bid accepted, we got rehab estimates that came in around $15,000-$20,000, which included adding another bedroom. Then we got an after-repaired value appraisal and it came in at $130,000. This was a screaming deal! We wholesaled it for $49,000, and it is still a great deal for our buyer. Even after the buyer makes all of the repairs they still have over $60,000 in profit left in the deal. Now I know they will have closing cost and holding costs, but this is still a great deal—and I also made over $20,000!

What If HUD Won't Go That Low?

I have had many people tell me over the years that HUD will not accept any offers less than say 80% or 82% or some number like that. HUD may have had a guideline at some point where they would not sell any property for less than 80% of market value, but if they do today I do not know about it and they are not sticking to it. I am actually glad that some people think this. It keeps them out of the market and from bidding against me.

We consistently buy houses that are a lot less than that, so if you have been told about some so-called minimum, take it with a grain of salt and make the offers anyway. You will learn from your personal experience.

If you make 40 or 50 offers using a certain formula and nothing comes of it, then at that point, try changing your formula. But give it a true test before you stop believing in it—not just a few offers. That's way too soon to tell. We make hundreds of offers a week and as of this writing, we have 34 houses under contract, but we had to make thousands of offers to get that many accepted, so don't give up.

My General Formula For Offers

In most markets, there is a price range that if you buy in you can't go wrong. Apply this to properties at the middle of the market down to the lower middle:

Offer no more than 70% of After-Repaired Value, minus repairs and closing costs. In fact, we start much lower, as you will soon see. This is the price at which it's hard to fail when buying properties to either fix up and resell or hold for the long term.

If you are buying this property to keep for yourself as a rental or lease option property, this is the most you will want to pay for it.

If you are wholesaling this property to someone else, this is the price they will pay for it. In this case, you need to buy it for less than this so that you can make the difference for putting the deal together. This is called your wholesale fee.

Note that by after-repaired value (ARV), I mean the price that the property could sell for when fixed up and in good condition to someone who is going to live in it. The tax assessors value is a general idea—give or take 20%—but the best way is to get your agent to do a CMA (comparative market analysis) for you or at least, initially, to pull some comps.

As for the tax value, it used to be that the tax value would be lower than the actual value, but in today's market the tax values are actually usually higher, as a rule of thumb.

So, for example, if your agent tells you a home could resell for $200,000 and it needs paint, carpet, a new roof, and some other items ($20,000), you would offer 70% of $200,000, then subtract your estimated repair cost of $20,000— and any closing cost if you want to figure that in too, which would leave you with a maximum purchase price of $120,000. I didn't subtract any closing cost in this example. We actually start much lower.

If you are looking to wholesale, I would start with an offer of around $100,000 or less and go up $1,000 each day to a maximum of $120,000.

SPECIAL BONUS

I have a simple software program that my team uses to make offers and analyze deals. I call it my **Ultimate Property Analyzer** software, and it can help you analyze any property faster, more accurately, and with more confidence than ever before. As the owner of this book, you can get if for free by simply going to **www.HUDHomesHalfOff.com** and entering access code "HUD1." I have even included a video tutorial that will show you exactly how to use it.

Making Your Offer Online

When it's time to make your offer, your agent (or you, if you're an approved agent) will click on "Submit an Offer" button at the bottom of the Property Details Page.

You will be asked to log in and enter your NAID Number. You'll be taken to the Bid Submission Page. Here, you will type in the purchase price you agree to pay and select that you are paying cash or applying for conventional or other financing not involving HUD/FHA. The agent's commission will be automatically calculated for you.

In the Closing costs section, enter zero dollars. And check *"Investor"* under purchaser type, not *"Owner Occupant"*—unless you are purchasing the property to live in.

One of the questions you will also have to answer is: If the seller does not accept this offer, can the seller hold the offer as a backup accepted offer or not?" Always select "Yes." It means that even if

HUD rejects your offer initially, they can come back and accept it at a future time. This keeps you from having to keep submitting offers as time goes by on the same property over and over again— although you can do that, too, as previously mentioned.

Your agent, or whoever is submitting the offer, will need to know your Social Security number if you are buying the property in your personal name, or your tax ID number if you are purchasing the house in a company name.

It's important that the company name is spelled correctly, consistent with actual documentation, like articles of organization that you may need to show later on. Pay attention to how you write it, as you will need to get it right when signing documents as well. That's all you do! You will get a chance to review all of the information and click "Confirm." It also gives you some terms and conditions to agree to.

Once your bid is submitted, you go to the "Bid Acknowledgement Page." Make sure to print this page or copy and paste the bid details into another document.

My agent will paste it into the spreadsheet and save it in Google Docs, naming it for the date the offer was made. The agent will get access to the bid details at HUD's site later, if needed.

A little trick we learned from an insider at HUD is when you get your bid confirmation, the last two digits in the confirmation indicates the number of total offers they have had on this property. For example, if the confirmation number is 88576304, then they have had four total bids submitted on this property.

When Will I Get An Answer?

The bidding process on almost every HUD home ends every night

at midnight. The next day, they will look at all the offers that have been submitted online for each property the day before.

This means that your offer is not being compared to someone else's offer from a few days ago or shopped around while you wait in suspense. In all likelihood, there is no competition unless someone else happened to bid on the same property as you did on the same day. Unless, of course, you are in a hot market.

HUD will either accept it or make a counteroffer. This is another reason I love investing in HUD Homes—no competition to worry about or factor in, as you would be dealing with when buying properties at foreclosure auctions. If your offer is rejected, it simply expires and you will not get any response from HUD.

It's also nice to get an answer back quickly without having to spend a lot of time following up and wondering what's going to happen. This is a government run process and the predictability makes HUD Homes a great strategy for time-strapped investors.

You will need to make a lot of offers to get one accepted, but with HUD's fast responses, you won't have to juggle too many deals in your radar for too long.

Your Earnest Money Deposit

When you're making offers on HUD homes, you will have to put up an earnest money deposit. If the purchase price is below $50,000 the earnest money will be $500, and if the purchase price is above $50,000 the deposit will be $1,000.

But you don't have to pay this at the time you submit your offer— only once it's accepted. Whew! This means you don't have to come up with $2,500 to make 5 offers in one week. Now there are some real estate agents that will tell you that they need an earnest money check before submitting the offer. We simply do not work with these agents.

If you get the offer accepted and submit the money but don't end up purchasing the house through some fault of your own, you will lose the $500. Remember, there is no inspection period when purchasing as an investor.

This is your biggest risk while making offers to buy HUD homes, and truthfully, there are times when you'll want to bail out before going through with the purchase.

You mitigate your risk quite a bit by making lower offers, which covers you in case there's some additional repairs that you don't find out about until later. This is why I teach to make your offers very low, the way we do.

So what happens if you make an offer, get one accepted, and then find out something's horribly wrong with the house, and you don't want to buy it? If this happened, it would be a surprise to everyone because the house has already had someone go through it and confirm its condition and estimate the repairs. But if it did, then in the worst case you would just walk away from your deposit and avoid purchasing a problem property. Just write it off as a cost of doing business. That's what we do.

Don't Cry Over Spilt Milk

Fear and worrying about losing your earnest money deposit is not anything to be concerned about, because it won't be happening often. Look at it as a cost of doing business. If you have to lose the occasional earnest money deposit to HUD while succeeding at buying other properties, life will still go on. You're still way ahead of the game!

You're running a business to make money here, after all! Most of the deals you do will be found without the upfront costs that you would typically have if you were to advertise and get motivated sellers calling you. So if the worst-case scenario comes true and you lose a $500 deposit, consider it your start-up costs—still not bad. We don't lose too many, but we do lose one every once in a while.

There are times, though, when the closing falls through, but not from any fault of your own. The most common reason is if the property's title is not clear, like with the home I mentioned earlier.

In these cases, it would be the seller's fault and their responsibility to get it cleaned up. Worst case, they can't close and they refund you your earnest money. But this is the only time you will get it back if the property doesn't close.

No Weasel Clauses

In the HUD contract you sign and submit with your offer paperwork once an offer is accepted, you can't have the typical weasel clauses you might add when making offers and negotiating with homeowners face-to-face, using your own written agreement.

For example, you can't add additional terms and clauses in the HUD contract asking for an inspection period, nor can you make an offer contingent upon you getting a satisfactory appraisal.

Basically, their process is what it is and you don't get to ask for exceptions that give you more leeway and control. So make sure your offers are structured the way we've covered it here. Make offers low enough, and it's hard to lose if they're accepted.

Tip: Start Out Making All Offers On Thursdays

Here is a technique that I have taught many of my students who are nervous about only having two business days to get all of the paperwork and deposit to HUD. When you only have two days it doesn't give you much time to perform any due diligence, especially if you also work a full time job. So here is what you do:

always submit your offers on Thursday. The reason for this is that you have two business days to respond if your offer is accepted, otherwise you will forfeit your earnest money deposit.

Generally, you want more time after your offer is accepted in order to go look at the property, gather more rehab estimates or any other due diligence. Some investors don't look at any properties in person until after an offer is accepted. We have gotten to the point that we do not look at any of them—period.

So if you make your offer on a Thursday, you will get the answer back from HUD the next day—on Friday. From that point, you have two business days to respond. But since Saturdays and Sundays don't count as business days, you won't have to have the contract and deposit to HUD until the end of the day on Tuesday of the following week.

This way, you'll then have four days to finish doing your due diligence and confirm that you want to proceed to the next step, whereas, otherwise, you would only have two days.

If you are nervous about getting an offer accepted and want to make sure you have enough time to get all of your due diligence done, this is a technique that you can use to give you a couple of extra days.

This is something that we used to do when we first started buying HUD houses; however, we now make many offers on HUD houses every day so we do not want to wait until Thursday to make all of our offers. In fact, I would like to tell you about a strategy we use now to make hundreds of offers a day on HUD houses.

How To Make An Offer On Every HUD House In Your State Every Day

Now, you are going to love this. Another strategy that my team and some of my advanced students also do is to just do a search for an entire state and make offers on all of the properties in that state every day. For example, currently in North Carolina there are a total of 90 HUD properties in the whole state that are available to investors. As long as we keep our offers low enough, we can literally make an offer on every property in the entire state every day. By keeping our offers low enough, we do not have to worry about getting too many accepted at a time. We also know that when we do get one accepted, it isn't just a deal—it's a steal!

Here is how it works. We do this using a virtual assistant. We have a virtual assistant log into **www.HUDHomeStore.com** every day and download the list of properties in NC and SC. She then uses the formula below to make an offer, through our Realtor, on every property on the list. We do not get many accepted; however, when we do, we know it's a bargain.

Here is a formula we use when making offers on properties in the entire state:

Mobile Homes:

Doublewides only (no single wides)

19-25% of list price

Condos/Townhouses:

2 bedroom + is ok for condos.

19-25% of list price

Single Family:

On 2 Bedrooms DO NOT go over 25%

$50,000 or less, offer 19-30% of list price

$50,001–$100,000, offer 30-40% of list price

$100,000 plus, offer 40-50% of list price

Our virtual assistant starts at the low end of the formula and goes up one percent per day until she reaches the maximum offer percentage. Now, in order for you to do this, you will have to have a good relationship with a Realtor who will either do this themselves, have an assistant do it, or you can do what I did and pay for the virtual assistant to do it for your Realtor.

I pay my virtual assistant $4.00 per hour and she lives in the Philippines. I found her on **www.bestjobs.ph.** Another good site for locating virtual assistants is **www.odesk.com**. Simply perform a search for the keywords "real estate" and you will find many virtual assistants that already know how to perform many real estate related tasks. Some of the tasks include:

- Taking calls
- Making calls
- Making offers
- Designing ads and flyers
- Posting ads on Craigslist
- Searching for ads on Craigslist
- Building your buyers' list
- Posting your properties on many real estate sites
- Managing your social media accounts

- Answering emails
- Pre-screening sellers or buyers
- Much more

You can find a virtual assistant for as little as $1.00 per hour on the sites previously mentioned. For a good one, you will probably end up paying between $3.00 and $5.00 per hour. This is still a great way to get someone working for you when you do not have much time to work your real estate business starting out.

SPECIAL BONUS

Spend three days with me: For three full days in a private, closed-door event, my team and I will personally teach our exclusive techniques for making money in this volatile and unpredictable market. We will introduce you to additional advanced techniques and strategies we are using to run circles around our competition right now—yes, even in today's market! Visit **www.HUDHomesHalfOff**.com and enter access code HUD1 to claim your two free tickets to see my team and I live at my next boot camp.

CHAPTER SIX:
What Happens After The Offer is Made?

After you make your offer, one of three things happens:

- Your offer is accepted

- Your offer is rejected (they do nothing)

- They make a counteroffer

If HUD Makes A Counter Offer

HUD rarely makes counter offers, so don't expect this to happen often. Because of this, HUD homes are different from other kinds of investing in that when you make your offer there won't be as much lowballing, countering, and negotiating back and forth afterward like you typically might expect when buying investment properties from an individual or through a Realtor on a bank owned property.

But if they make a counter offer, you can either come back with a slightly higher price or stay firm where you are. However, if the numbers work, you could accept their counter offer.

Check your numbers again and increase your bid only if you're certain you'll still have a desirable profit when you're done and that your market value and repair estimates are accurate.

If HUD Rejects Your Offer

If your offer is rejected, don't worry about it. There are plenty of other deals out there for you to find, and remember, this is a numbers game. The more offers you make, the more chance you have of getting a deal.

You may have to make 40, 50, or even 100 offers before one is accepted. So really, the name of the game is seeing how quickly you can make an offer—not only in terms of hours or days but how much time you spend working on it.

With the bidding and submission process as easy as it is, there's no excuse not to crank out offers quickly. You have nothing to lose, and making offers on HUD homes alone is not a full-time job.

A good way to motivate yourself to make enough offers is to set a goal of how many you'll make in the next month, week and per day. Then keep a tally of how many you make on a piece of paper or in some way that you will be constantly reminded of your goal and can track your progress. You can use my spreadsheet that I have included as a bonus with this book, as previously mentioned.

Take a little time to celebrate each time you make an offer, and it won't seem like such a long distance until you get your deal. Celebrate the small victories.

If HUD Accepts Your Offer

If your offer is accepted, then your agent will have received an e-mail notifying them that the offer has been accepted. Attached to the e-mail will be the contract package containing several items of paperwork that you must sign and send back to them.

The cover page mentions the closing attorney's name that HUD will be using and the expiration date for the offer.

You'll see the sales contract, some extra addendums about mold and other things that are self-explanatory, and a pamphlet for you, as required by law. It will also explain HUD's forfeiture and extension policy and guidelines for your earnest money, which we have already covered.

Sign these in blue ink (yes, at the time of this writing you really do have to sign using a blue pen—black will not suffice) and send it back along with your earnest money and proof of funds letter if you are financing the purchase.

If you are qualifying for a mortgage, you will have had to submit an application to your lender already and will have received a pre-qualification letter. This will give you a good amount of confidence, knowing in advance that you can get the financing you will need to fund your purchase.

When making offers, having a pre-approval letter looks stronger than having a pre-qualification letter because the financing is more certain. A pre-approval means that you have submitted documentation that verifies the information submitted on your application. This way the lender knows you can actually qualify. A pre-qualification letter is the same thing except it is subject to the lender verifying all of the information that you submitted on your application.

The easiest way to get a proof of funds letter is from a hard money lender or transaction funding lender if you are purchasing the property for investment. Also, a transaction funding lender is a lender that will loan you the money to be able to close on the transaction so you can sell it to your buyer immediately. These funds are used when you are wholesaling a property to another investor the same day as you bought it.

A hard money lender is used when you will be buying the property to fix it up yourself. They typically charge a higher interest rate and points; however, it is a lot cheaper than having to bring in a partner. Once you are approved, they will write a verification on their letterhead saying something to the effect of "You are approved for a loan of up to 70% of the after-repaired value of a qualifying properties' value," or something similar.

My good friend, Wendy Sweet, is a hard money lender and she actually works in the same office as I do. She only does loans for investors in North and South Carolina at this point, but she is the best in the business. If you live in the Carolina's or want to buy a property as an investor in the Carolina's, then you should contact her. Her website is **www.CarolinaHardMoney.com**.

If you were bidding on short sales or other listed properties, it would be a bigger deal regarding how specific and solid your proof of funds letter is. But there's no "credibility factor" in HUD's process for accepting offers. They accept or reject offers based on price alone, not how solid your financing is.

If you are paying cash, a bank statement or snapshot of your bank balance can prove that you have the funds to close. You can also provide something proving that you have a line of credit to draw from. We will cover a lot more on financing in a future chapter.

Walkthrough Of The Contract Package And Forms

For your convenience, this section will show you the paperwork package currently required to fill out when submitting an offer on a HUD Home and a brief explanation of each item.

You can download the entire packet in PDF format from the Addendums tab on the Property Details page for any HUD home listed for sale at **www.HUDHomeStore.com**

The first item is the instructions for filling out the Sales Contract. This shows a line-by-line breakdown of the questions on the sales contract you'll fill out to submit your offer.

After that, you will see a blank copy of the Sales Contract as you would fill in the blanks in real life, followed by its second page, a reiteration of the conditions and guidelines you are acknowledging that you understand and commit to follow. Examples of these are shown on the following pages.

Instructions for
Sales Contract
Property Disposition Program

U.S. Department of Housing
and Urban Development
Office of Housing
Federal Housing Commissioner

OMB Approval No. 2502-0306
(exp. 3/31/2001)

This collection of information is required in order provide a binding contract between the property purchaser and HUD.

The public reporting burden for this collection of information is estimated to average 30 minutes per response, including the time for reviewing instructions, searching existing data sources, gathering and maintaining the data needed, and completing and reviewing the collection of information.

Responses to the collection are required in order to administer the Property Disposition Sales Program (24 CFR 203.375, 24 CFR 203.278, 24 CFR 291.100-291.30).

The U.S. Housing Act of 1937, as amended, authorized the Department of Housing and Urban Development (HUD) to collect all the information on this form.

The Housing and Community Development Act of 1987, 42 U.S.C 3543 authorized HUD to collect Employer Identification Number and/or Social Security Number. These numbers are used to provide information to the IRS regarding payment of commissions or other fees. HUD may also disclose this information to Federal, State and local agencies when relevant to civil, criminal, or regulatory investigations and prosecutions. It will not be otherwise disclosed or released outside of HUD, except as required and permitted by law. Failure to provide the Employer Identification Number or Social Security Number could affect your participation in HUD's property disposition program.

HUD may not conduct or sponsor, and a person is not required to respond to a collection of information unless it displays a currently valid OMB control number.

This Sales Contract, identified as form HUD-9548, must be prepared and transmitted in accordance with the following instructions. The form provides an original for fiscal and legal review, signed copy for the Purchaser, and unsigned information copies for the Purchaser, the selling Broker, and HUD's designated representative.

Remove this Instruction Sheet and type the HUD Case Number in the box in the upper right.

Item 1: Type Purchaser(s) name and complete property address.

Item 2: Enter name(s) and style in which title will be taken.

Item 3: Enter Bid Amount and amount of earnest money Purchaser has deposited.

Enter holder of earnest money deposit in accordance with Seller's instructions.

Item 4: Enter when appropriate, strictly in compliance with Seller's offering. If Seller has offered the property with insured financing available, and Purchaser is buying under such means, check the first block and the applicable type of insured financing, and complete the down payment and mortgage information. If the insured mortgage involves a repair escrow (and has been so offered by Seller), also check the appropriate block and insert the amount of the repair escrow.
Note: The amounts shown for "cash due at closing" and "balance by mortgage" do not include the FHA Mortgage Insurance Premium, prepaid expenses or closing costs Seller has agreed to fund into the mortgage.
Note: If Purchaser is paying cash or applying for conventional or other financing not involving FHA, check appropriate block.

Item 5: Enter amount of financing/closing costs Seller is expected to pay.
Note: If the amount stated in Item 5 exceeds actual and typical allowable financing and/or closing costs, such excess shall not be paid by Seller and may not be used by Purchaser to reduce amount(s) owing to Seller.

Item 6: Enter dollar amount Seller is expected to pay, including any selling bonus if offered by Seller. The commission will be paid by Seller upon completion of closing.

Item 7: Enter net amount due Seller (purchase price [Item 3], less Items 5 and 6). Contract will be awarded on the basis of the greatest acceptable net return to Seller.

Item 8: Enter appropriate occupancy information. If left blank, Purchaser will be considered as an investor. If purchaser qualifies for discount, enter percent. Discount will be reduced by amounts, if any, on Line Items 5 and 6. (Do not enter discounted price on contract.)

Item 9: Enter in accordance with HUD's instructions.

Item 10: Enter appropriate back-up offer information.

Item 11: Enter if an addendum is to be attached to and made a part of this contract.
Note: Addendum not previously approved by Seller may not be made a part of this Contract. Approved addendum must be signed by, and in the same style as, those signing as Purchaser(s).

Item 12: Purchaser(s) must initial in appropriate space.

Other: a. Failure of the Purchaser to perform in accordance with this contract may cause the Seller to retain all or a portion of the earnest money deposit. Broker must be certain this is fully explained to and understood by the Purchaser(s).
b. Enter Selling Broker's Name and Address Identifier (NAID). If broker has not been issued a SAMS NAID, complete forms SAMS-1111, Payee Name and Address, and SAMS-1111-A, Selling Broker Certification, along with required documentation, and attach to this contract. Contact HUD's local designated representative.
c. The Broker is required to inform Purchaser of the Conditions of Sale on the reverse of the Sales Contract, and particularly of Purchaser's right and responsibility for satisfying itself as to the full condition of the property prior to submitting an offer to purchase and that Seller will provide no warranty or perform any repairs after acceptance of the Contract.

Signatures: Sign Original, leaving carbon inserts intact, making certain that the signature(s) appears on all copies.

Transmittal: Forward the Original with Copies 1 and 2 to HUD's designated representative. Copies 3 and 4 are to be retained by Broker and Purchaser as information copies. Upon acceptance, HUD's designated representative will return the signed Copy 1 to Broker for delivery to Purchaser(s). HUD's designated representative will retain Copy 2.

Sales Contract
Property Disposition Program

U.S. Department of Housing and Urban Development
Office of Housing
Federal Housing Commissioner

RED Case No. _____

1. I (We), _____

   (Purchaser(s)) agree to purchase on the terms set forth herein, the following property, as more particularly
   described in the deed conveying the property to the Secretary of Housing and Urban Development:

   _____

   (street number, street name, unit number, if applicable, city, county, State)

2. The Secretary of Housing and Urban Development (Seller) agrees to sell the property at the price and terms set forth herein, and to prepare a deed
   containing a covenant which warrants against the acts of the Seller and all claiming by, through or under him. Title will be taken in the following
   name(s) and style: _____

3. The agreed purchase price of the property is ....▶ **3. $** _____
   Purchaser has paid $ _____ as earnest money to be applied on the purchase price, and agrees
   to pay the balance of the purchase price, plus or minus prorations, at the time of closing, in cash to Seller. The
   earnest money deposit shall be held by _____

4. ☐ Purchaser is applying for FHA insured financing (☐ 203(b), ☐ 203(b) repair escrow, ☐ 203(k)) with a cash
   down payment of $ _____ due at closing and the balance secured by a mortgage in the amount of
   $ _____ for _____ months (does not include FHA Mortgage Insurance Premium,
   prepaid expenses or closing costs Seller has agreed to fund into mortgage.).
   ☐ Said mortgage involves a repair escrow amounting to $ _____
   ☐ Purchaser is paying cash or applying for conventional or other financing not involving FHA.

5. Seller will pay reasonable and customary costs, but not more than actual costs, nor more than paid by a typical Seller
   in the area of obtaining financing and/or closing (excluding broker's commission) in an amount not to exceed ..▶ **5. $** _____

6a. Upon sales closing, Seller agrees to pay to the broker identified below a commission (including
    selling bonus, if offered by seller) of _____ **6a. $** _____

6b. If broker identified below is not the broad listing broker, broad listing broker will receive a commission of:▶ **6b. $** _____

7. The net amount due Seller is (Purchase price [Item 3] less Items 5 and 6) ....▶ **7. $** _____

8. Purchaser is: ☐ owner-occupant (will occupy this property as primary residence) ☐ investor
   ☐ nonprofit organization ☐ public housing agency ☐ other government agency. Discount at closing: _____ %
   Discount will reduced by amounts, if any, listed on Line Items 5 and 6.

9. Time is of the essence as to closing. The sale shall close not later than _____ days from Seller's acceptance of contract. Closing
   shall be held at the office of Seller's designated closing agent or _____

10. If Seller does not accept this offer, Seller ☐ may ☐ may not hold such offer as a back-up to accepted offer.

11. Lead based paint addendum ☐ is ☐ is not attached. Other addendum ☐ is ☐ is not attached hereto and made part of this contract.

12. Should Purchaser refuse or otherwise fail to perform in accordance with this contract, including the time limitation, Seller may, at Seller's sole option,
    retain all or a portion of the deposit as liquidated damages. The Seller reserves the right to apply the earnest money, or any portion thereof, to any
    sums which may be owed by the Purchaser to the Seller for rent. Purchaser(s) initials: _____ Seller's initials: _____

13. This contract is subject to the Conditions of Sale on the reverse hereof, which are incorporated herein and made part of this contract.
    Certification of Purchaser: The undersigned certifies that in affixing his/her/its signature to this contract he/she/it understands:
    (1) all the contents thereof (including the Conditions of Sale) and is in agreement therewith without protest; (2) he/she/it is responsible
    for satisfying itself as to the full condition of the property; and (3) that Seller will not perform repairs after acceptance of this contract.

Purchaser(s) (type or print names & sign)	Purchaser(s) Address:
Purchaser(s) Social Security Number (SSN) or Employer Identification Number (EIN) (include hyphens)	Phone No:	Date Purchaser(s)Signed Contract:
Seller: Secretary of Housing and Urban Development By: (type name & title, & sign) X		Date Contract Accepted by HUD:

Certification of Broker: The undersigned certifies that: (1) neither he/she nor anyone authorized to act for him/her has declined to sell the
property described herein to or to make it available for inspection or consideration by a prospective purchaser because of his/her race, color,
religion, sex, familial status, national origin, or disability; (2) he/she has both provided and explained to the purchaser the notice regarding use
of Seller's closing agent; (3) he/she has explained fully to the purchaser the entire terms of the contract, including Condition B on the reverse hereof;
and (4) he/she is in compliance with Seller's earnest money policy as set forth on HUD forms SAMS-1111, Payee Name and Address, and SAMS-
1111-A, Selling Broker Certification, which he/she has executed and filed with Seller.

Broker's Business Name & Address: (for IRS reporting) (include Zip Code)	Broker's EIN or SSN: (include hyphens)	SAMS NAID:
	Signature of Broker: X	Broker's Phone No.

Type or print the name and phone number of sales person: _____

This section for HUD use only. Broker notified of:	Authorizing Signature & Date:
☐ Acceptance ☐ Back-Up No. _____	
☐ Rejection ☐ Return Earnest Money Deposit	X

Previous editions are obsolete.   ref. Handbook 4310.5   form HUD-9548 (1/99)

Conditions of Sale

A. All assessments, including improvement assessments which are available for payment without interest or penalty for advance payment, taxes, rent, and ground rent, if any, shall be prorated as of the closing date.

B. Seller makes no representations or warranties concerning the condition of the property, including but not limited to mechanical systems, dry basement, foundation, structural, or compliance with code, zoning or building requirements and will make no repairs to the property after execution of this contract. Purchaser understands that regardless of whether the property is being financed with an FHA-insured mortgage, Seller does not guarantee or warrant that the property is free of visible or hidden structural defects, termite damage, lead-based paint, or any other condition that may render the property uninhabitable or otherwise unusable. Purchaser acknowledges responsibility for taking such action as it believes necessary to satisfy itself that the property is in a condition acceptable to it, of laws, regulations and ordinances affecting the property, and agrees to accept the property in the condition existing on the date of this contract. It is important for Purchaser to have a home inspection performed on the property in order to identify any possible defects. If FHA insured financing is used, up to $200 of the cost to perform the inspection may be financed into the mortgage. Names of home inspection companies can be found in the yellow pages of your telephone directory under the heading "Home Inspection Services."

C. If financing is involved in this transaction (Item 4), Purchaser agrees that should he/she/it fail to provide documentation indicating that proper loan application was made in good faith within 10 calendar days of the date this contract was accepted by Seller, and/or thereafter otherwise to put forth good faith efforts to obtain necessary financing, Seller shall have the option of rescinding this contract and retaining all or a portion of Purchaser's earnest money deposit.

D. Seller may rescind this contract and return all or a portion of Purchaser's earnest money deposit under the following conditions:
1. Seller has not acquired the property.
2. Seller is unable or unwilling to remove valid objections to the title prior to closing.
3. Seller determines that purchaser is not an acceptable borrower.
Tender of the deposit shall release the Seller from any and all claims arising from this transaction.

E. Purchaser may not perform repairs nor take possession of the property until sale is closed. Risk of loss or damage is assumed by Seller until sale is closed, unless Purchaser takes possession of the property prior thereto, in which case State law shall apply. (1) If sale involves FHA insured financing and after damage the property no longer meets the intent of Minimum Property Standards (MPS), Seller may, at its option, perform repairs or cancel the contract and return Purchaser's full earnest money deposit. If, after damage, the property still meets the intent of MPS, Purchaser has the option of accepting the property as-is, with a purchase price adjustment at Seller's sole discretion, or cancelling the contract and receiving refund of full earnest money deposit. (2) If sale does not involve FHA insured financing, Seller will not repair damage but may, at Seller's sole discretion, reduce the sale price. Purchaser has option to cancel the contract and receive refund of full earnest money deposit. Tender of the earnest money shall release Seller from any claims arising from this transaction.

F. If this property is being offered with FHA insured mortgage financing available, Seller's acceptance of this contract constitutes a commitment to insure, conditioned upon Purchaser being determined by Seller or Direct Endorsement Underwriter to be an acceptable borrower and further conditioned upon Seller's authority to insure the mortgage at the time the sale is closed.

G. Purchaser understands that Seller's listing price is Seller's estimate of current fair market value.

H. No member of or Delegate to Congress or Resident Commissioner shall be admitted to any share or part of this contract or to any benefit that may arise therefrom, but this provision shall not be construed to extend to this contract if made with a corporation for its general benefit.

I. Purchaser and Seller agree that this contract shall be binding upon their respective heirs, executors, administrators, successors or assigns but is assignable only by written consent of the Seller.

J. If this property was constructed prior to 1978, Seller has inspected for defective paint surfaces (defined as cracking, scaling, chipping, peeling or loose paint on all interior and exterior surfaces). Seller's inspection found no defective paint surfaces, or if defective paint surfaces were found, Seller has treated or will treat such defective surfaces in a manner prescribed by Seller prior to closing. **Purchaser understands and agrees that the Seller's inspection and/or treatment is not intended to, nor does it guarantee or warrant that all lead-based paint and all potential lead-based paint hazards have been eliminated from this property.** Purchaser acknowledges that he/she it has received a copy of a pamphlet which discusses lead-based paint hazards and has signed, on or before the date of this contract, the Lead-Based Paint Addendum to Sales Contact - Property Built Before 1978. Purchaser understands that the Lead-Based Paint Addendum must be signed by all Purchasers and forwarded to Seller with this contract. Contracts which are not in conformance with these requirements will not be accepted by Seller.

K. The effective date of this contract is the date it is accepted (signed) by the Seller.

L. If the amount stated in Item 5 exceeds actual and typical financing and/or closing costs, such excess shall not be paid by Seller and may not be used by Purchaser to reduce amount(s) due Seller.

M. Seller's policies and requirements with regard to earnest money (including forfeiture thereof), extensions of time in which to close the sale, back-up offers, and allowable financing and/or closing costs are detailed in instructions issued to selling brokers.

N. Seller makes no representations or guarantees that the property will, in the future, be eligible for FHA insured mortgage financing, regardless of its condition or the repairs which may be made.

O. Warning: Falsifying information on this or any other form of the Department of Housing and Urban Development is felony. It is punishable by a fine not to exceed $250,000 and/or a prison sentence of not more than two years. (18 U.S.C. 1010, 3559, 3571)

P. This contract contains the final and entire agreement between Purchaser and Seller and they shall not be bound by any terms, conditions, statements, or representations, oral or written, not contained in this contract.

Previous editions are obsolete   ref. Handbook 4310.5   form HUD-9548 (1/99)

84   Visit **www.HUDHomesHalfOff.com** to claim your bonuses

This next addendum acknowledges that you're submitting your bid electronically (online), that you understand your responsibilities, and certify that nothing has been falsified.

Case #

Electronic Filing of HUD-9548 Contract Addendum

Purchaser(s) and Broker have elected to use the HUD-9548 contract form electronically downloaded and printed for the submission of their bid _____ (confirmation number) for case # _____.

By doing so, all parties to this agreement certify, warrant, and represent that no information and/or content of the HUD-9548 contract has been altered or omitted in any manner. They further certify, warrant, and represent that this is a true and accurate copy of the HUD-9548 contract.

The broker and purchaser(s) further agree that (i) they read and understand their responsibilities, as stated in the "Conditions of Sale," which is a part of the HUD-9548 Sales Contract and (ii) no contract or binding agreement exists unless and until a written HUD-9548 Sales Contract, executed by the U.S. Department of Housing and Urban Development is returned to purchaser.

The broker and purchaser(s) knowingly execute this addendum with full understanding that "falsifying information on this or any other form of the Department of Housing and Urban Development is felony. It is punishable by a fine not to exceed $250,000 and/or a prison sentence of not more than two years (18 U.S. C. 1010, 3559, 3571)."

CERTIFICATION OF ACCURACY

The following parties have reviewed the information above and certify to the best of their knowledge it is true and accurate, and that they agree to all of the terms and provisions hereof.

_____   _____
Purchaser   Date

_____
Print Name (Purchaser)

_____   _____
Purchaser   Date

_____
Print Name (Purchaser)

_____   _____
Broker/Agent   Date

_____
Print Name (Broker/Agent)

This next form does not need to be filled out. It is just a statement telling you what your rights are and why you may want to get a home inspection prior to purchase, and what to test for.

CAUTION

U.S. Department of Housing
and Urban Development
Federal Housing Administration (FHA)

OMB Approval No: 2502-0538
(exp. 07/31/2009)

For Your Protection:
Get a Home Inspection

Why a Buyer Needs a Home Inspection

A home inspection gives the buyer more detailed information about the overall condition of the home prior to purchase. In a home inspection, a qualified inspector takes an in-depth, unbiased look at your potential new home to:

- ✔ Evaluate the physical condition: structure, construction, and mechanical systems;
- ✔ Identify items that need to be repaired or replaced; and
- ✔ Estimate the remaining useful life of the major systems, equipment, structure, and finishes.

Appraisals are Different from Home Inspections

An appraisal is different from a home inspection. Appraisals are for lenders; home inspections are for buyers. An appraisal is required to:

- ✔ Estimate the market value of a house;
- ✔ Make sure that the house meets FHA minimum property standards/requirements; and
- ✔ Make sure that the property is marketable.

FHA Does Not Guarantee the Value or Condition of your Potential New Home

If you find problems with your new home after closing, FHA can not give or lend you money for repairs, and FHA can not buy the home back from you. That is why it is so important for you, the buyer, to get an independent home inspection. Ask a qualified home inspector to inspect your potential new home and give you the information you need to make a wise decision.

Radon Gas Testing

The United States Environmental Protection Agency and the Surgeon General of the United States have recommended that all houses should be tested for radon. For more information on radon testing, call the toll-free National Radon Information Line at 1-800-SOS-Radon or 1-800-767-7236. As with a home inspection, if you decide to test for radon, you may do so before signing your contract, or you may do so after signing the contract as long as your contract states the sale of the home depends on your satisfaction with the results of the radon test.

Be an Informed Buyer

It is your responsibility to be an informed buyer. Be sure that what you buy is satisfactory in every respect. You have the right to carefully examine your potential new home with a qualified home inspector. You may arrange to do so before signing your contract, or may do so after signing the contract as long as your contract states that the sale of the home depends on the inspection.

HUD-92564-CN (6/06)

CAUTION

Visit **www.HUDHomesHalfOff.com** to claim your bonuses

HUD Homes Half Off!

You will fill out and turn in this next addendum if you intend to buy the property as an owner-occupant and live in it as your personal residence. I strongly suggest that you never try to deceive HUD, your agent, and the title company if you are not truly buying it for this purpose. This is fraud and you could go to jail.

Addendum to the Sales Contract
Property Disposition Program

U.S. Department of Housing
and Urban Development
Office of Housing
Federal Housing Commissioner

OMB Approval No. 2502-0306
(exp. 09/30/2008)

Warning: Falsifying information on this or any other form of the Department of Housing and Urban Development is a felony. It is punishable by a fine not to exceed $250,000 and/or a prison sentence of not more than two years.

Individual Owner-Occupant Certification

I/we, _____
submit this offer to purchase the property located at

Property address: _____

as an owner-occupant purchaser. I/we certify that I/we have not purchased a HUD-owned property within the past 24 months as an owner-occupant. This offer is being submitted with the representation that I/we will occupy the property as my/our primary residence for at least 12 months.

Purchaser's
Name,
Signature & Date: _____

Purchaser's
Name,
Signature & Date: _____

Broker Certification

I certify that I have not knowingly submitted the HUD-9548, Sales Contract, for the above listed property, on behalf of an investor purchaser. I further certify that I have discussed the penalties for false certification with the purchaser(s).

Broker's
Name,
Signature & Date: _____

ref. Handbook 4310.5   form HUD-9648-D (1/98)

This next form explains the rules and nuances regarding your earnest money deposit and what happens if you fail to close. Make sure that you take this seriously and understand your rights and the consequences of not closing on time or not closing at all.

Forfeiture of Earnest Money Policy

All HUD Property Disposition sales of HUD-acquired properties are to close within 20 days acceptance of a HUD-9548 Sales Contract offer to purchase cash.

All HUD Property Disposition sales of HUD-acquired properties are to close within 45 days acceptance of a HUD-9548 Sales Contract offer to purchase with financing.

Forfeiture of Earnest Money Deposit

The failure by a Purchaser to close on the sale of property within the allowable time period, including any extensions granted by HUD, will result in the forfeiture of the earnest money deposit, except where special circumstances exist and are documented and accepted by HUD.

Investor Purchasers

- **Uninsured Sales** – The purchaser will forfeit 100% of the earnest money deposit for failure to close, regardless of reason.

- **Insured Sales** – The purchaser will forfeit 50% of the earnest money deposit for failure to close if purchaser is determined by HUD or Direct Endorsement underwriter to be an unacceptable buyer. The purchaser will forfeit 100% of earnest money deposit if sale fails to close for any other reason.

Owner-Occupant Purchasers

- The purchaser will have 100% refund of the earnest money deposit under the following circumstances:

    1. There has been a death in the immediate family (contract holder, spouse, or children living in the same household);
    2. There has been a recent serious illness in the immediate family that has resulted in significant medical expenses or substantial loss of income, thus adversely affecting the purchase's financial ability to close the sale;
    3. There has been a loss of job by one of the primary breadwinners, or substantial loss of income through no fault of the purchaser;
    4. On an insured sale, HUD or a Direct Endorsement underwriter determines that the purchaser is not an acceptable borrower;
    5. On an uninsured sale, the purchaser was pre-approved for mortgage financing in an appropriate amount by a recognized mortgage lender and , despite good faith efforts, is unable to obtain mortgage financing in a specified dollar amount sufficient to purchase the property
    6. For other good cause, as determined by the field office.

- On an uninsured sale, the purchaser will forfeit 50% of the earnest money deposit where, despite good faith efforts by the purchaser, there is an inability to obtain a mortgage loan from a recognized mortgage lender.

- On either type of sale, the purchaser will forfeit 100% of the deposit in those instances where no documentation is submitted, where the documentation fails to provide an acceptable cause for the buyer's failure to close, or where documentation is not provided within a reasonable time following contract cancellation. The documentation must be received by HomeTelos, LP no later than close of business on the tenth day following cancellation of contract.

Buyer Certification:

I/we acknowledge that I/we have been interviewed, completed a loan application and received a Pre-Qualification Letter from an approved lender.

Signatures

_____   _____
(Purchaser)   (Purchaser)

_____   _____
(Purchaser)   (Purchaser)

Rev 100510

This next document, shown on the following page, explains your rights to request for an extension if for some reason you can't close on the property within the promised time frame.

Keep in mind that HUD is not guaranteeing that they will allow an extension just because you ask for one. They approve these on a case-by-case basis, so do all you can to get your financing lined up in advance so this does not happen except in rare occasions.

Note that there are also fees to pay each day that the closing is delayed. They're not exorbitant, but can get into the hundreds if things slide 5 to 10 days. We have done this and continue to do this, if needed, when our buyer is not ready to close. I would rather pay a couple hundred dollars to delay the closing instead of paying for the entire property and holding it until my buyer closes with me. Trust me; you will understand this policy when you're selling houses yourself!

Closing Date Extension Policy

If closing date stipulated in the contract cannot be met, purchasers may request an extension of the closing. Extensions of time to close the sale are at the Seller's discretion and, if granted, will be under the following guidelines:

1. The request for extension of closing time will be made in writing to the designated HUD Closing Agent for processing. The request must include the cause of delay and that necessary mortgage funding has been obtained or is imminent. A signed and dated lender letter should be received by HUD's Closing Agent prior to expiration of the sales contract.

2. Extensions will be granted for a 15 calendar day period. The following are the extension fees due to the Closing Agent at the time of submission of extension request. These fees must accompany the extension request and be a non-refundable certified or cashier's check or money order in the full amount of the 15 day extension.

This fee is based on the Contract Sales Price:

Contract Sales Price of $25,000 or less	Extension Fee is $10 per day
Contract Sales Price of $25,001 to $50,000	Extension Fee is $15 per day
Contract Sales Price over $50,000	Extension Fee is $25 per day

3. At the time of closing, the unused extension fees, if any, will be prorated to the Purchaser.
4. The granting of an initial extension period does not obligate Seller to grant additional extensions.
5. Extension fees will be retained by Seller if a closing does not occur.

Buyer Certification:

I/we have read and understand this policy and agree to abide by the above policy.

Signatures:

_____   _____
(Purchaser)   (Purchaser)

_____   _____
(Purchaser)   (Purchaser)

The next two pages are a form HUD has you sign to make sure that they have disclosed everything to you about the condition of the property. They are not agreeing to do any repairs to the house and you are buying it as-is.

PURCHASER'S RIGHTS AND RESPONSIBILITIES
Addendum to HUD-9548 Sales Contract

FHA CASE NO.: _____

PROPERTY ADDRESS: _____

PRINTED NAME(S) OF PURCHASER(S): _____

_____

CONDITION OF PROPERTY

HUD makes no representations or warranties concerning the condition of this property, including, but not limited to, mechanical and operating systems (electrical, plumbing, sewage, kitchen appliances, heating and air conditioning), dry basement, roof, structural condition, or compliance with local codes, zoning, or building requirements.

HUD will authorize NO repairs to this property. The prohibition of repairs, regardless of the nature or severity of a defect or code violation, extends to all latent (unknown) defects or code violations discovered at any time, including after the closing date. Purchaser(s) are fully responsible for satisfying themselves as to the full condition of this property and any laws, regulations or ordinances affecting this property.

THE IMPORTANCE OF A HOME INSPECTION

HUD does not warrant the condition of a property. It is important for you to have a home inspection performed on the property you wish to purchase in order to identify any possible defects. Up to $200 of the cost to perform the inspection may be financed into your FHA mortgage.

15-DAY CONTRACT CANCELLATION CONTINGENCY FOR CONTRACTS OWNER OCCUPANT

Owner Occupant Purchaser(s) may request that the Sales Contract be canceled if, within 15 days of HUD's acceptance, the property is inspected by a professional home inspector who discovers a structural, roof, system defect, or non-compliance with local codes, zoning, or building requirements that were not previously disclosed and HUD elects not to correct, or if within such 15 day period, the property is inspected for the presence of radon by a professional radon inspector to an extent unsatisfactory to you. **A copy of the property inspection report, or radon test report, as applicable, must be attached to the cancellation request.**

The cancellation contingency is limited to structural, roof, defective components within the mechanical and operating systems (which include the electrical, plumbing, sewage, heating and air conditioning systems only) or noncompliance with local codes, zoning, or building requirements. Kitchen appliances, window air conditioner units, light fixtures, receptacles and switch covers are not included in the operating systems. Equipment age or energy efficiency ratings are not included in the cancellation contingency. The earnest money deposit will be returned to owner occupant purchasers ONLY if HUD concurs with the home inspection report finding(s).

OTHER IMPORTANT INFORMATION

The purchaser has the right to make a final inspection of this property 24 hours prior to closing. This is an "as-is" sale and HUD will not make any repairs. Failure to close may result in forfeiture of earnest money. In case of credit denial, all or part of the earnest money may be refunded. It is the broker/agent's responsibility to submit the credit denial letter to HomeTelos, LP, within ten business days. Failure to do so will result in forfeiture of all earnest money. Closing agents will not release funds until processing is completed by the HUD office. Extensions must be requested before expiration of the contract. Extension fees are non-refundable. I acknowledge that I am not allowed to occupy or make repairs to the property prior to closing. If I am employed by the U.S. Department of Housing and Urban Development (HUD), or if I am related by blood, marriage, or law to a HUD employee, I must have prior approval before signing a HUD sales contract.

Buyer should have an Abstract covering the property examined by an attorney of Buyer's selection or Buyer should be furnished with or obtain a Title Policy. If a Title Policy is to be obtained, Buyer should obtain commitment for Title Insurance (the Commitment) which should be examined by an attorney of Buyer's choice at or prior to closing. All locks should be replaced or re-keyed at Purchaser's expense.

HUD'S LISTED PRICE
PURCHASER(S) MAY BID ABOVE OR BELOW HUD'S LISTED PRICE. HUD'S ORIGINAL LIST PRICE WAS BASED UPON AN APPRAISAL. PURCHASER(S) ACKNOWLEDGE THAT HUD'S LISTED PRICE OF THIS PROPERTY IS $_____. (_____) Buyer's Initials

The above information was explained to the purchaser(s) by:

_____
Signature of Broker/Agent Date

I/We acknowledge receipt and understanding of the "PURCHASER'S RIGHTS AND RESPONSIBILITIES" addendum.

_____ _____ _____ _____
Signature of Purchaser   Date   Signature of Purchaser   Date

_____ _____ _____ _____
Signature of Purchaser   Date   Signature of Purchaser   Date

Lastly, there's an addendum for you to read over and acknowledge that you understand the property may have mold or radon gas.

They have you sign this for every home, and it doesn't mean your particular deal is more or less likely to have these toxic items. Just know that it might, and that a thorough inspection by a professional will uncover them prior to closing.

**Radon Gas and Mold Notice
and Release Agreement**

U.S. Department of Housing
and Urban Development
Office of Housing
Federal Housing Commissioner

Property Case #: _____

Property address: _____

_____

_____

_____

PURCHASERS ARE HEREBY NOTIFIED AND UNDERSTAND THAT RADON GAS AND SOME MOLDS HAVE THE POTENTIAL TO CAUSE SERIOUS HEALTH PROBLEMS.

Purchaser acknowledges and accepts that the HUD-owned property described above (the "Property") is being offered for sale "AS IS" with no representations as to the condition of the Property. The Secretary of the U.S. Department of Housing and Urban Development, his/her officers, employees, agents, successors and assigns (the "Seller") and _____,

insert name of M & M Contractor

an independent management and marketing contractor ("M & M Contractor") to the Seller, have no knowledge of radon or mold in, on, or around the Property other than what may have already been described on the web site of the Seller or M & M Contractor or otherwise made available to Purchaser by the Seller or M & M Contractor.

Radon is an invisible and odorless gaseous radioactive element. Mold is a general term for visible growth of fungus, whether it is visible directly or is visible when barriers, such as building components (for example, walls) or furnishings (for example, carpets), are removed.

Purchaser represents and warrants that Purchaser has not relied on the accuracy or completeness of any representations that have been made by the Seller and/or M & M Contractor as to the presence of radon or mold and that the Purchaser has not relied on the Seller's or M & M Contractor's failure to provide information regarding the presence or effects of any radon or mold found on the Property.

Real Estate Brokers and Agents are not generally qualified to advise purchasers on radon or mold treatment or its health and safety risks. **PURCHASERS ARE ENCOURAGED TO OBTAIN THE SERVICES OF A QUALIFIED AND EXPERIENCED PROFESSIONAL TO CONDUCT INSPECTIONS AND TESTS REGARDING RADON AND MOLD PRIOR TO CLOSING.** Purchasers are hereby notified and agree that they are solely responsible for any required remediation and/or resulting damages, including, but not limited to, any effects on health, due to radon or mold in, on or around the property.

In consideration of the sale of the Property to the undersigned Purchaser, Purchaser does hereby release, indemnify, hold harmless and forever discharge the Seller, as owner of the Property and separately, M & M Contractor, as the independent contractor responsible for maintaining and marketing the Property, and its officers, employees, agents, successors and assigns, from any and all claims, liabilities, or causes of action of any kind that the Purchaser may now have or at any time in the future may have against the Seller and/or M & M Contractor resulting from the presence of radon or mold in, on or around the Property.

Purchaser has been given the opportunity to review this Release Agreement with Purchaser's attorney or other representatives of Purchaser's choosing, and hereby acknowledges reading and understanding this Release. Purchaser also understands that the promises, representations and warranties made by Purchaser in this Release are a material inducement for Seller entering into the contract to sell the Property to Purchaser.

Dated this _____ day of _____, 20___.

_____   _____
Purchaser's Signature   Purchaser's Signature

_____   _____
Purchaser's Printed Name   Purchaser's Printed Name

Form HUD-9548-E (6/2004)

More Paperwork

There will be more documents depending on the deal, the age of the property, the state the property is located in and other factors. There may be a Lead Based Paint disclosure, an Attorney Preference Disclosure and/or Insurance Preference Disclosure or any of a number of other documents. Your real estate agent will have them if there are any others required by HUD, so don't worry about having to create any of your own documents.

What If There Is A Mistake In The Paperwork?

If for whatever reason you find out that the paperwork you submitted with your offer was filled out incorrectly, your agent can log in as a bidder and make or request the necessary changes.

Ideally, you will find and correct changes before HUD gets back to you, so your contract has a chance to be accepted that day. It may be that the buyers' name was incorrect or different in the print than in the signature, or was signed with black ink, or whatever.

Worst case, the change will not be accepted and your contract will be turned down. In this case, HUD will put the property back on their website for bids, so you simply resubmit your offer the next day online just like before and you will have another chance to be the winning bidder. We have had to do this several times for one reason or another.

Also, sometimes your paperwork will go through an agent at HUD who overlooks things or thinks you did something wrong on the paperwork even when you did not.

They'll kick these back to you, reject your written contract, and refund your earnest money deposit to you. The house goes back on the market, and you lose nothing. So it's not the end of the world, but you should just expect it to happen from time to time if you're doing multiple deals.

Your Realtor can ask for that person's supervisor and ask them to re-examine the offer and package, and hopefully, they will accept it.

Sometimes mistakes are made like this with no rhyme or reason. HUD is overwhelmed and sometimes things slip through the cracks, or perhaps the person assigned to the file is new and made a mistake.

Due Diligence

Once you get the property under contract and all of the paperwork has been sent into HUD, now it is time to start your due diligence. I call due diligence "separating facts from opinions." What I mean by this is, although a Realtor or someone else has told you what the after-repaired value will be, what the neighborhood is like, or what the repairs may run, *due diligence is* when you get validation from professionals and from doing your own research, as we will cover in this section.

Below are the things we do to perform our due diligence. We will go through each one of them one at a time. We do not always do all of these on every property. You will have to decide which methods of due diligence that you do. For example, if we are going to get three rehab estimates and an after-repaired value (ARV) appraisal, then we may not get a comparative market analysis (CMA).

Online Comps

There are many websites that you can go to for what we call online comps. These are websites like **www.Cyberhomes.com**, **www.Zillow.com**, and **www.Eppraisal.com**. All of these sites can give you a valuation of what they think the value of the property is. This is a good indicator; however, it will not always give you an accurate valuation. For example, Zillow is known for giving values that are higher than actual values. So for this reason I do not use Zillow for their value estimation; I use them only to find out the property sales history and sales history of similar properties.

When I use Zillow, I look up the "sold" properties similar to the property I am buying. That way, I see actual properties that have already sold and what they sold for instead of relying on what Zillow says they think it is worth.

Neighborhood Analysis

The next thing you will want to do is to look at the neighborhood. Remember, you should stay out of the "war zones," as a lot of people call them. These are areas that have high crime rates and high unemployment. All cities of any decent size have these kinds of areas.

When you are buying out of town or out of state from where you live, it is important to know the type of neighborhood the property is in since you may not be familiar with the city or state. For this research I use websites like:

www.CrimeReports.com,
www.ZipSkinny.com,
www.SpotCrime.com
www.NeighborhoodScout.com.

In doing your neighborhood analysis it is also important to ask a lot of questions to everyone you talk to about the property as well. When you are talking to Realtors, home inspectors, rehab contractors and appraisers, always ask them what they think of the neighborhood.

Some of the questions I ask a Realtor when I get them on the phone is:

- How much work does it need?

- How long has it been on the market?

- Have you had many offers?

- How is the market there?

- Would this be a better rental property or better as a fixer upper to retail?

- Do you get many listings like this?

- Do you have any other properties I need to make an offer on today?

- Let me tell you a little about what we do...

- The realtors we work with on a regular basis love us because...

- Do you mind if I get your email address so we can stay in touch and I can buy more houses from you?

- Do you have an automatic email notification list you could put me on to get new listing alerts?

Rent Comps

If you are either going to rent out your HUD home or you are going to sell it to someone who will rent it out, it is important to know the potential rent that can be expected from the property.

For this we also ask the Realtor, but we also use sites like **www.RentoMeter.com** and **www.HotPads.com**.

Most landlords expect at least one percent per month in rents, but in today's market I expect at least two percent and try to get as close as I can to three. The higher the price of the property the harder it is to do this.

To figure out what one percent per month would be, simply take the cost you will have in the property then multiply it by .01. For example, if you have a total of $50,000 invested in a property after you purchase it and make the necessary repairs, then one percent would be $500 per month in rents.

Comparative Market Analysis (CMA)

A Comparative market analysis (CMA) is done by a real estate agent to determine the possible selling price in order to come up with a listing price for the potential seller. They basically look at similar sold properties in the area to determine what they think your property will sell for. A CMA is a good indication of what a property will sell for; however, it is not as detailed as an appraisal.

Contractor Estimates

As previously mentioned, HUD has their own Property Condition Report or (PCR), which you can download from their website; however, I suggest you get your own as well.

You can get a rehab contractor to give you an estimate for making any necessary repairs. You can find one in any area, in any state, by going to a website like **www.ReliableRemodeler.com,**

www.NeedContractor.com or www.ServiceMagic.com. These are a few of the websites we use to find reputable contractors.

These websites basically have contractors apply to get listed on their website so they can get leads of people who are wanting to have repairs and improvements done to their homes. The contractors are typically pre-screened. They are also licensed, bonded and insured; the lead generating websites mentioned above usually require this. Once you go to the website and enter your project, there are three contractors who will receive your contact information and job description that you posted on the website.

Because the contractors are paying for your contact information they are usually fast at getting in touch with you. We usually get a call within minutes. We have found some of our best contractors on these websites.

One of the things we usually tell the contractor is whether or not this property will be repaired to be used as a rental or as a property that will be retailed to a new owner occupant. We do this because you remodel a house differently depending on what you will be doing with it. For example, if a house was a fairly nice home and we planned on retailing it, we may put in granite counter tops. However if it was a rental property, we would probably use a laminate counter top.

After-Repaired Value (ARV) Appraisal

You may want to get an appraisal performed, depending on what you will be doing with the property. If you will be wholesaling it or retailing it, then you will be getting an appraisal. You will be getting an ARV, or After-Repaired Value, appraisal done. Also, if you are getting any kind of financing done by a lender, then they will be ordering an appraisal.

An appraisal is done by a licensed appraiser. You can find one by asking the real estate agent or by going to a site like **www.AppraisalLoft.com** or **www.AppraisalInstitute.org**. If you are getting financing from a lender such as a rehab loan (better known as a hard money loan), or a FHA 203k loan, they will order their own appraisal to determine the value of the property once repaired.

HUD may have already had a home appraisal done, but it is rare that you can use the existing one as your own if you are qualifying for a loan. Your lender will want their preferred appraiser to give his opinion, and will order a new one to ensure that the results are recent and done by one of their approved appraisers.

If you are going to keep the property as a rental and are paying cash then you may or may not even order an appraisal. The choice is up to you. However, if you are just getting started investing in real estate, you may want to get an appraisal done just to validate the value before you close.

Home Inspection

You could also get a Home Inspection if you wanted to. A Home Inspection is performed by a licensed home inspector. You can find them in any city in any state by going to **www.AmericanHomeInspectorDirectory.com** or by asking any local Realtor. They usually have a short list of home inspectors that they have worked with in the past.

The home inspectors primary job is to identify any safety issues. They will tell you this; however, they are also able to identify any items that either do not work or will need to be replaced or repaired in the near future.

We do not typically get a home inspection done unless it is a very expensive house and we want to make sure that our rehab contractors didn't miss anything in performing their rehab estimates.

Larry Goins

CHAPTER SEVEN:
Financing Options For You Or Your Buyer

Each of the financing options discussed in this section has its different costs, timeframes to fund, terms, and pros and cons. You want to know your exit strategy in order to choose which financing type you'll be using. This is why you'll want to pick the method you're going to use before you make the offer in the first place. We will be discussing exit strategy in the next chapter, which is all of the different ways to make money on your HUD home.

Prepare For Your Financing Up Front

If you are getting financing, you will need to get that ball rolling right away to avoid a delay. You also need to stay on top of it throughout the whole process to ensure that you close on time. Check in with your loan officer or the person handling your loan at least once per week. It takes about 30 days for a typical loan to go through the process and get to closing, so it pays to be sure of your financing at the time you're making your offer. However, as you will see, there are other types of funding that can be done very fast, especially for investors.

What If I Need More Time To Close?

Typically, if you don't complete the transaction within the time frame given to you, you will lose the property, forfeit your deposit money, and it will go back up for bid. The time frame in which you promise to close must be entered on the HUD sales contract. Now this applies to investors. Owner-occupied buyers have a little more flexibility, but not much.

You can request an extension of time, and these are granted on a case-by-case basis. The Extension Request form needs to be submitted by the Broker, regardless of the reason for the delay.

Make sure to do this within 5 days of the scheduled closing date, and it helps to include a letter from your lender stating that the financing can still go through—which is HUD's biggest concern.

Your Own Sources Of Funds

Many people already have sources they can tap into to fund their HUD home. You may have the money in the bank, and if so, that is great. You may also have accessible funds available on your credit card or on a home equity line of credit or even on a personal line of credit, for example. All of these can be used to fund your HUD home purchase short term. You will, however, want to either sell the property or refinance it once you get it repaired.

Private Lenders

Private lenders, like partners, are people in your network of personal contacts with the funds to lend, but who agree to be paid a fixed interest rate as their return.

A typical deal might go like this:

You find a house you can buy for $50,000. You need $12,000 for repairs, and figure another $4,000 for closing costs, title insurance, and the utilities, signs, and other marketing you will do to get the property sold over a few months.

Add all these up and $66,000 is the grand total you need to do this deal without coming out of pocket yourself. Then, let's say you agree to pay this lender 15% simple interest. On a $66,000 loan, this comes up to $825 per month in interest that is due every month if you structured the loan to be paid monthly.

When borrowing from private lenders always get them to fund 100% of the deal, including repairs! Otherwise, what are they good for? They're supposed to bring money to the table and you do the rest. By doing this, you can do an unlimited number of deals without running out of cash or having any hang ups along the way. The last thing you want is to get stuck with a property halfway renovated without the rest of the funds needed to finish the job.

Most private money lenders will want to be paid monthly; however, you may be able to structure it so that your lender allows you to pay them once the property is sold. If you are borrowing money from a private lender, this is an ideal situation as you will not have to worry about making payments on the loan and can pay back the interest and principal when you sell the property. Unless they are living off the interest payments, most private lenders should be able to wait six months to make their money back again. But also keep in mind that they want to get paid back as quickly as possible (and so do you), so don't let the lack of payments allow you to become un-motivated and let the months slip by before the house is rehabbed and sells.

How To Find All The Private Money You Will Ever Need

A great way to find private money lenders is to go to your local Real Estate Investors Association. You can find one near you at **www.NationalREIA.com**. Simply find out when their next meeting is and attend it. Ask around for who is doing a lot of real estate deals. Once you find them, ask them who they use for financing. If they say they use private money, ask them for a business card. Once you have their company name, you can go to the court house in your county and go to the Register Of Deeds office and look up the properties they have purchased. Once you find that, look to see who the lender is that will be listed on the mortgage—THERE IS YOUR PRIVATE LENDER! Think about it, if the lender will loan other investors money, why wouldn't they loan you money as well. This is a great strategy that not many people know about. You could ask the investor themselves, but they will probably not tell you.

Partners

Partners are people who have enough available cash to purchase the property, let you find it and oversee the renovation, and then split the money that is made when it sells.

You can find these for long-term deals as well, but most people want their money back soon and can't sit on a deal forever.

You would not pay them any interest, but you would pay them some percentage of the grand total made from the deal—it all depends on what you negotiate!

A 50-50 split is pretty fair, if you have to, but try for around 25% if you can get them to accept it.

Compared to other financing options, you are going to have to give away a piece of the deal, which may represent $10,000 or $20,000. But the expression is true that it's better to have *part of something* than *all of nothing* if you cannot get qualified to get financing on your own. You're still making more than a wholesale deal and bypassing the unpredictability of getting mortgages.

You can, however, also use this method of funding when wholesaling as well. In fact, if you use a partner when wholesaling, they will get their money back even faster.

A good source to find partners is to ask your friends or relatives if they would be interested in partnering with you for a percentage of the profits.

If you are reluctant to do that or do not have any friends or relatives that have money, then you can try a source like **http://www.fundingpost.com** or **http://www.gobignetwork.com** or **http://www.go4funding.com.**

Hard Money Lenders

Hard money lenders are a different kind of mortgage lender, with loans that are more expensive but much easier to qualify for as an investor. They make their loans based on the equity in the property more so than they care about your credit score, income, job, etc. However, in today's market they do want to make sure you can qualify by having good credit, income and some reserves in the bank to help make the payments.

To give you an example of a hard money loan, if a property is worth $200,000, they might loan up to $130,000 or $140,000. They know that if you fail to fix it up and repay the loan on time that they are still in a position to take the property back, put it on the market themselves, and get their money back. Often, they are investors themselves or have a network of investors to take the property off their hands if anything goes wrong. So long story short, your credit score does not have to be as high and they can also get you the funding in a week or two if need be.

And they typically don't make you jump through as many hoops as much as regular mortgage companies, whose rules and standards are constantly changing—the borrower who qualifies one month may not be able to get a loan the next. And, hard money lenders typically don't require you to make a down payment on the property, which is a big plus because down payments are a huge waste of capital. Use your cash to do repairs instead, or go for a no-money-out-of-your-pocket deal.

You can find a list of hard money lenders in your state by Googling "hard money lenders" and your state's name. There is also a network of hard money lenders that help to match lenders with borrowers. You can find them at **www.hardmoneyagent.com.**

If you are in the Carolina's you can use my good friend, Wendy Sweet, who is more knowledgeable than anyone I know about finance. She has an office in my office building in Lake Wylie, SC so I see her every day. You can check out her website at **www.CarolinaHardMoney.com.** She is very good at helping investors.

Transactional Funding

If you plan to wholesale the property and buy it and sell it the same day, there is a type of funding called transaction funding. This type of funding is used to fund the purchase of your HUD home just long enough to close with your buyer the same day and get your money back. This type of funding can only be used when buying and selling very fast, such as wholesaling.

Transaction funding lenders will also give you the POF, the "Proof of Funds" letter you need to be able to submit cash offers on HUD homes. When using this type of funding, it is very important that you have your buyer lined up and ready to close on the same day that you are closing on your purchase of the property from HUD. To get a list of all of the transactional funding lenders that offer this type of funding simply go to **www.HUDHomesHalfOff.com** and enter access code HUD1.

Personal Credit Lines

Credit cards and lines of credit can even be used to buy HUD homes. Believe it or not, some homes have been bought so cheap that they are financed with one or more credit cards. This happens in a lot in states with very depressed real estate values or when you get a screaming deal on a property.

You can also use credit cards to come up with your $500 earnest money deposit, a down payment (if your lender will allow it), or the repair money you need for a fix and flip. If your credit card limits are not that high, you may have a personal line of credit or home equity line of credit on your personal residence. With these, you are approved once and can then write checks or withdraw funds to do deals as needed without having to qualify again or get permission.

It's hard to beat the flexibility *lines of credit* offer you—to be able to write your own check at closing without jumping through a lot of hoops, or being able to fund your repair costs in addition to your purchase price. Just make sure that you still do your due diligence and proceed with the same caution and conservative offers you would make if you had to convince a lender why this deal is going to work.

Business Line of Credit

If you have a business entity, you probably get offers in the mail for business lines of credit and company credit cards. It might surprise you how high of a limit you can get by filling out a simple one-page application.

Just remember, if they are paying to send you mail it means you are on a list of companies they already suspect are good candidates for their loans.

You can improve your business credit just like your personal credit in order to qualify for more. The easiest way is to get a business account from somebody like Fed-Ex or Staples.

Just get a business line of credit of any amount you can and make payments on it consistently for a few months. Often, they will contact you again announcing that they have increased your limit by $10,000 or sometimes up to 100%.

Peer To Peer Lending Sites

There are websites that specialize in lending money on an unsecured basis. Basically, the website matches individuals with people needing to borrow money. The borrower may be requesting funding for any purpose. They may be wanting to consolidate their bills, buy a car, remodel their home or any other purpose.

The borrower applies and posts their request, indicating how much interest they are willing to pay. Then, other individuals commit to lending a specific amount, say $50 - $100 each. Once all of the loan amount has been reached, the borrower gets the money (minus a fee for the peer to peer website) and makes payments to the website company, which is then transferred to the lenders who put up the money.

You can typically borrow up to $25,000 and sometimes more. The main websites that offer this type of funding are **www.LendingClub.com** and **www.Prosper.com**.

Self-Directed IRA Or Retirement Account

A lot of people do not even know this but you can actually buy real estate and lend money on real estate using your IRA or retirement account. I have been doing this for years. It is a great source to fund your deals. Basically, anyone with an IRA or retirement account can change custodians to a self-directed custodial.

Special Bonus

I have put together an audio training and special report that will teach you exactly how to set this up just like I have it done. You can get the special report and audio training by going to **www.HUDHomesHalfOff.com** and enter access code HUD1.

Traditional Financing For Owner-Occupied Buyers

There are several financing options available for owner-occupants to choose from, just as there are for investors—each with their own set of pros and cons. A seasoned mortgage broker or loan officer is usually your best bet for getting the right financing to buy a personal residence.

Loan officers are the folks who pull your credit to see which types of loans you qualify for, how much you can borrow, how much you will have to put down, etc. They work with various banks, mortgage companies, and other lending institutions to find you the best loan program.

A mortgage broker is a loan officer who can help to make loans for a variety of financing companies, not just one. The biggest downside to using a local bank or a single company like Washington Mutual to get a mortgage is that they only have a limited number of programs available, and they might have criteria that are higher than other lenders' who might make a better loan to the same borrower.

The best way to find a good loan officer or mortgage broker is to ask some Realtors and your friends and personal network who they have used with success. You can also ask other investors or look up mortgage brokers online to see who is in your town.

First-Time Homebuyer And FHA Financing

One of FHA's highest priorities is to help people to purchase their first home. They define a first-time homebuyer as an individual who meets any of the following criteria:

- An individual who has had no ownership in a principal residence during the 3-year period ending on the date of purchase of the property. This includes a spouse (if either meets the above test, they are considered first-time homebuyers).

•A single parent who has only owned with a former spouse while married.

•An individual who is a displaced homemaker and has only owned with a spouse.

•An individual who has only owned a principal residence not permanently affixed to a permanent foundation in accordance with applicable regulations.

•An individual who has only owned a property that was not in compliance with state, local or model building codes and which cannot be brought into compliance for less than the cost of constructing a permanent structure.

HUD has helped many people become homeowners through FHA financing. To get an FHA loan you have to work with a bank or lender that offers FHA financing. It is offered to first time homeowners as described previously.

FHA guidelines are easier to qualify for than traditional lenders loans, since FHA is insuring the loan. This means that if the borrower defaults then HUD will step in and pay off the loan for the lender and then foreclose on the property as mentioned at the beginning of this book. I have seen borrowers qualify for an FHA loan who didn't have any credit references on their credit report. This happens because the guidelines allow you to "build" a credit reference by contacting the borrower's creditors that may not be reporting to the credit bureau. The reference and pay history from that creditor is used to help the borrower qualify.

Down Payment Assistance Programs

For those who qualify, the American Dream Down Payment Initiative assists low-income, first-time homebuyers in purchasing single-family homes by providing funds for their down payment, closing costs, and repairs carried out along with the home purchase.

The down payment assistance can't exceed $10,000 or 6% of the purchase price of the home—whichever is greater. And the rehab work must be completed within one year of your purchase.

Ask your loan officer if you're eligible for this program when you're getting pre-qualified for FHA financing.

Nonprofits used to be able to offer down payment assistance and the seller could pay for it but that has ended. Now only the government is able to offer down payment assistance and the seller can't pay for it.

FHA's 203(k) Loan Program

The purchase of a house that needs repairs is often a catch-22 situation, because a traditional bank won't lend the money to buy the house until the repairs are complete, and the repairs can't be done until the house has been purchased.

HUD's 203(k) program can help you with this and allow you to purchase or refinance a property, plus include in the loan the cost of making the repairs and improvements. The FHA insured 203(k) loan is provided through approved mortgage lenders nationwide. It is available only to persons wanting to occupy the home.

The down payment requirement is approximately 3.5% of the acquisition and repair costs of the property.

The 203(k) loan includes the following steps:

A potential homebuyer locates a fixer-upper and executes a sales contract after doing a feasibility analysis of the property with their real estate professional. The contract should state that the buyer is seeking a 203(k) loan and that the contract is contingent on loan approval based on additional required repairs by the FHA or the lender.

The home buyer then selects an FHA-approved 203(k) lender and arranges for a detailed proposal showing the scope of work to be done, including a detailed cost estimate on each repair or improvement of the project. The appraisal is performed to determine the value of the property after renovation.

If the borrower passes the lender's credit-worthiness test, the loan closes for an amount that will cover the purchase or refinance cost of the property, the remodeling costs and the allowable closing costs. The amount of the loan will also include a contingency reserve of 10% to 20% of the total remodeling costs and is used to cover any extra work not included in the original proposal.

At closing, the seller of the property is paid off and the remaining funds are put into an escrow account to pay for the repairs and improvements during the rehabilitation period.

The mortgage payments and remodeling begin after the loan closes. The borrower can decide to have up to six mortgage payments (PITI) put into the cost of rehabilitation if the property is not going to be occupied during construction, but it cannot exceed the length of time it is estimated to complete the rehab.

Escrowed funds are released to the homeowner during construction through a series of draw requests for work that is completed. To ensure completion of the job, 10% of each draw is held back; this money is paid after the homeowner informs the lender that the work has been completed and after the lender determines there are no additional liens on the property.

This type of loan used to be offered to investors, but because of many unethical investors who inflated repair costs and values it was discontinued for investors some years ago.

You can get a list of lenders who are offering the 203(k) Rehabilitation Program here:

http://www.hud.gov/ll/code/llslcrit.cfm

CHAPTER EIGHT:
How To Make Money From Your HUD House

In this section we will cover the different ways you can make money with your new HUD home purchase. We are going to cover the four most popular options—the ones you will probably be using if you are getting started in investing.

Several exit strategies available are:

1. Wholesaling the deal to another investor who will fix it up and flip it or keep it as a "buy and hold" investment.

2. Buy & Hold the house as a rental property.

3. Flipping is where you buy the house, fix it up, and sell it for a short-term profit to an owner-occupant for full market value.

4. Sell with Seller Financing to another investor or first time home buyer.

Wholesaling HUD Properties

There is a strategy known among real estate investors called *wholesaling*. This is an ideal way for beginners to begin making money even without cash and credit of their own.

When you wholesale a deal, you find a property and negotiate a contract with a seller for a low price. In this case, you make an offer on a HUD home and get an offer accepted with them.

Then, instead of qualifying to get the financing yourself and buying the house on your own, you will find another real estate investor who can pay cash for it (either they have the cash or they have access to quick funding) and let him buy it instead for a little more than your contract price. You get to keep this difference as your fee for putting the deal together.

So, for example, if your offer is accepted by HUD for $80,000 and you find an investor willing to buy it for $85,000, then you would sign a contract to sell the house to that person and close on the same day as your closing to buy it. I call this "real estate day trading."

The attorney or title company will then conduct what is called a *simultaneous closing*, where you will buy and sell the same property within an hour's time or so.

Before this can happen, your buyer will deposit his money, (whether it's his own money or his funding sources money) with the attorney or title company, who will then use it to pay your purchase price and to pay the money owed to HUD.

You never have to come up with the money yourself, HUD sells a property for the agreed-upon price, and an investor in town gets a great deal on a property that he can keep or fix up and sell himself. Sounds like a win/win/win!

Now this can be tricky when trying to line up your closing with your buyer's closing for the same day. In fact, some attorneys or title companies do not allow you to close on this type of transaction if you do not have the funds to bring to closing. In this case you will simply use a transactional funding lender as previously described.

The other thing about wholesaling is, because you are finding cash buyers to take the property, they are able to close faster than someone who must qualify for a loan. This means your payday is even faster!

Many real estate investors choose to only wholesale their deals, making relatively smaller chunks of profit for investing their time and expertise scanning the market for homes and making a lot of offers.

To wholesale a deal, you need to be networking with serious real estate investors in your area. Meet them in advance and find out what kind of properties they're looking for and where they are getting the money from so you will not be wasting your time working with someone who has no money. When you have a handful (some investors may have relationships with hundreds or thousands), then you have a group of people you can announce new deals to by e-mail as they arrive.

Building Your Buyers' List

The most important thing you need when wholesaling is a buyers' list. Without a buyers' list you could get stuck with a property, and you do not want that. You should always be looking to build your buyers' list. There are many different ways to find wholesale buyers and here is a list:

•Going to foreclosure auctions and getting business cards from the bidders.

•Calling the numbers on all "I Buy Houses" signs and ads that you see around town.

•Look in the "real estate wanted" section of your newspaper's classifieds and all online classifieds as well.

•Look in the "For Sale" and "For Rent" sections as well—you can often tell they are investors if they use phrases like "lease option" or "seller financing."

•Networking at your local real estate investors association. You can find them at **www.NationalREIA.com.**

•Finding out who bought the properties that you bid on but lost—check the tax records to see who the new owner is and their contact information.

•Run ads on sites like **Craigslist.com** and **Backpage.com** that say you have deep discounted properties for sale and to contact you to get on your buyers' list.

•Put out your own signs that say "Handyman Specials" Cheap, Cash! with your phone number.

There are many websites you can go to in order to build your buyers' list. In fact, below is a list of all of the major websites you can use to find buyers for your wholesale deals. They are also a good source to find properties as well.

Here are the real estate specific sites:

http://www.propbot.com

http://www.postlets.com

http://www.trulia.com

http://www.zillow.com

http://www.propertysites.com

http://www.owners.com

http://agent.point2.com/,

http://www.submityourlistings.com/

http://www.nationalhomesearch.com/

http://www.realestate.com/

http://www.newhomesource.com/

http://www.allthelistings.com/

http://realestate.shop.ebay.com/

http://www.virtualfsbo.com/

http://www.forsalebyowner.com/index-home.php

http://www.byowner.com/index.html

http://www.forsalebyownercenter.com/

http://www.homesbyowner.com/

http://www.homeportfoliojunction.com/index.htm

http://www.fsboadvertisingservice.com/

http://www.fsbo.com/

http://www.buyowner.com/

http://www.houselocator.com/default.aspx

http://www.homefinder.com/

http://hotpads.com/

http://soldbyowner.com/

http://www.postyourhome.com/page.php

http://www.vflyer.com/main/Guest.jsp

Following are the free online classified sites that are not necessarily real estate specific:

http://www.ibidfree.com/

http://www.classifiedsforfree.com/

http://www.hyt.com/

http://www.usfreeads.com/

http://www.inetgiant.com/

http://www.azfamily.com/marketplace/classifieds/

http://epage.com/js/epmain.jsp

http://www.backpage.com/

http://www.worldslist.com/us/

http://realestate.oodle.com/

http://www.livedeal.com/index.jsp

http://www.craigslist.org/

http://www.vast.com/

http://realestate.yahoo.com/

http://www.kaango.com/

http://www.olx.com/

http://www.hoobly.com/

http://www.ebayclassifieds.com/

http://www.webclassifieds.us/

http://www.bestwayclassifieds.com/

http://www.kijiji.com

> ### Special Bonus
>
> Wholesaling is the main way my team and I buy and sell 10 to 15 or more deals per month—and most of our properties are sold the same day we buy them. In other words, we line up our closing when we are buying for the same day when we are selling. So we literally close on buying the property and right after we own it, we close on selling it. I call this *real estate day trading*. Buying and selling houses the same day. For more information on how I run my operation, visit **www.HUDHomesHalfOff.com** and enter access code HUD1. Here, you can watch a training video I have prepared for you that details the whole process.

Can I Assign My HUD Contract When Wholesaling?

When wholesaling houses the same day, there are generally two main ways to structure the transaction—double closings and assigning the contract.

Being able to assign a contract is the easiest way to wholesale a property. You may be asking, what is assigning a contract anyway? When assigning a contract, you are actually just selling the paperwork instead of the property. You simply get the property under contract to purchase in the name of "your name AND OR ASSIGNS" so you can simply assign your contract to your buyers and do not have to come up with the money to purchase the property and then resell it. You use a document called an "Assignment of Contract" that states that you are assigning your interest in the contract to your buyer for a fee. This fee would be your wholesale profit.

As is the case with buying homes repossessed by banks (REO's), you cannot assign your interest in your contract to buy a HUD home to someone else for a fee. They will not allow it.

Instead, simultaneous or double closings are the best way to get the job done. You already have your contract to buy (from HUD), so now you will sign a new contract to sell the property to your investor buyer.

In a simultaneous closing, the second closing will take place on the same day as the first, and the buyer's funds will be used to give to HUD. Choosing the right title company to represent you is the key to this process. Make sure you find one that is familiar and comfortable with double closings. HUD will choose their title company to represent them, and you choose yours to represent you if you want. Many investors use their own title company. In order to do a simultaneous or double closing, you would need to use the same attorney or title company for both transactions.

We have been buying so many properties that the HUD attorneys know us well and know what we do, so we just use them and not another to represent us too.

You can also get it under contract to buy in a land trust and assign the beneficial interest in the trust to your cash buyer at closing. I have also seen it done by buying the property from HUD in the name of a brand new LLC and then selling the LLC to your cash buyer. These are a couple of ways to assign a non-assignable contract.

Your attorney or title company can help you with this type of transaction. Although it can be done, it is not done often. There are other ways to get the funding to be able to close on buying and selling the same day without using these specific techniques.

Both of these will require you to educate your buyer a little bit on the process. If it gets too complicated or your buyer won't cooperate, find another buyer or just do a double closing using one of the funding methods earlier described.

To see how I personally announce and resell my wholesale properties, or to get notified of deals my team has for sale, just go to **www.HUDHomesHalfOff.com** and enter access code HUD1." I have a link to a a special video there just for you so you can get on my VIP buyers' list to get advanced notification of my wholesale properties.

Buy And Hold Properties

Keeping real estate and renting it to tenants for several years or more is a well-known strategy and probably the most common. The advantages are that you can make a lot more money in the long run from the cash flow from the rent a tenant will pay.

You also increase your equity over time as the loan is paid down (if you have a loan), as market values increase, and you may also receive depreciation benefits on your tax return.

The downside to buying and holding is that the financing is harder to get and you have to wait longer for your payday—sometimes years longer. If you have the money to put down, are qualified for a mortgage, and don't mind managing the property and tenants over the years, this may be the way to go. The benefits are that you are building long term passive income and equity in the property, which is an asset you can always keep forever or eventually sell.

Many investors also pay cash or get short-term financing in order to buy a property in a couple of days or weeks, and then refinance with a loan whose interest rate is lower than it would be getting an initial purchase money loan.

If buying and holding is your strategy, do your market research and find out what areas of your city or state are scheduled to have the most appreciation, or, are in the path of progress. Those are the places you'll want to look for homes during your search. You can use **www.Google.com** to find out this information. Simply search for the keywords: "your state" then "cities with best appreciation." Example: "South Carolina cities with best appreciation."

I think every investor should keep at least a few properties as rentals. This way you are building long-term wealth. If all you ever do is wholesaling or flipping then you will always have a "job." This is because flipping and wholesaling is a business and keeping properties as rentals is an investment.

I also think that every investor should learn how to deal with tenants and manage properties. You may not like it, but it is good experience to learn how to do it. When I keep a property as a rental, I like to try and get at least 2-3% per month of what I have in the property as rent. For example, if I paid $25,000 for the property and invested another $5,000 in repairs then I have a total investment of $30,000. Well, 2-3% of that per month would be $600-$900 per month in rents. This is not a bad return on my investment when you multiply this by 12 to get my annual yield. But remember, you will have repairs and maintenance and vacancies from time to time.

The other good news is you will also have other tax advantages of owning real estate, such as depreciation.

Many of the investors who purchase properties from me keep them as rentals since we have such great deals at deep discounts. Go to

www.HUDHomesHalfOff.com and enter access code HUD1 to get on my VIP buyers' list. I will put you on my advanced notification list to get notified of my properties before the general public. I have a video I have prepared for you that describes my advanced notification VIP buyers' list. Check it out and you may want to create a video similar to this for your buyers' list also.

Flipping Houses

"Flipping" is another way of saying, "buy it, fix it up, put it on the market, and sell it again." There are many shows on TV that are focused on this one method. This works by buying properties under market value and getting them in excellent shape again so they can sell for as much as the market will bear. Your profit can be $10,000 to $30,000 or more—depending on how good of a deal you got when you purchased and also depending on the market value of the homes you are fixing up.

Flipping homes is a short-term strategy for those who want to get paid in a matter of months. It typically takes three to six months to fix up a home, market it properly, show it to buyers, and get one of them to the closing table with their financing. It takes longer because you are selling it for retail to someone who will live in the property, so they will be a little more particular. Remember, someone who either has cash or can qualify for a loan can choose any home they want, so it may take some time to sell yours.

The main advantage of flipping houses is that you make your money in a short period of time, not sometime down the road when the future is less certain. The main downside, though, is that it's harder to find a qualified retail buyer than a tenant.

When we decide to retail a property and sell it retail, we typically list it with a Realtor. We also usually offer a bonus to the selling agent. This can be between $500 and $5000. This money goes directly to the Realtor or agent who brings the buyer. This is an incentive for the Realtors to show your home more than they do

others. We also sometimes offer a free gift to a buyer like a big screen TV or new riding lawn mower for an acceptable offer. It also helps when selling a house at retail to offer to pay the buyers closing costs. You may have a buyer interested in buying your home, but they may only have enough money for their down payment but not the closing costs. This can make them choose your home over another they are considering.

What Are The Seasoning Requirements Before I Can Resell?

It used to be that a retail buyer could not get an FHA loan to buy a property unless the previous owner (You) had held title to the property for at least 90 days.

This was an effort meant to prevent fraud, but was a big nuisance to legitimate house flippers who wanted to resell again quickly. And to make matters worse, the vast majority of homebuyers have used FHA financing since 2007 or so, so it was a real impediment for a while.

Fortunately, on February 1, 2010, HUD waived this requirement in order to help more people get affordable housing, and it has been that way ever since. This is great news for investors, who no longer have to keep their funds needlessly tied up in vacant inventory, waiting 90 days before they can sell if their buyer is using FHA to finance the property.

Sell With Seller Financing

You could also sell your HUD home with seller financing to either an investor who will fix it up and rent it out or to a buyer who wants to fix it up to live in it.

You can either make the necessary repairs or sell it to the buyer "as is" and let them make the repairs. That is what we do when we sell one of our properties with seller financing. This is a great way to get long term cash flow without having the problems associated with property management.

Basically, when you finance a property for your buyer you are acting as the bank. The buyer will be making regular monthly payments to you just like they would if they got their financing through a bank or mortgage lender. It is very important that you qualify your buyer when offering seller financing. You want to make sure they can handle the payments and that they are a good credit risk for you.

The more down payment they put down the better for you. There are many ways you can structure your seller finance transaction. I typically finance our properties for ten years at 11% interest rate. I try to get at least five percent down payment from my buyer. This helps to keep defaults to minimum. The key to getting great returns is not necessarily the interest rate but the difference in price from what you paid for the property and what you are selling it for. I try to sell my properties that I am seller financing for at least 3-6 times what I paid for them.

Special Bonus

We have a strategy that allows us to capitalize on seller financing by buying dirt-cheap houses that no one else wants, and then sell them for 3-6 times what we paid by selling them with seller financing. We have gotten returns from 119% to 788% on our investment by receiving monthly payments and getting paid more over time. This is a great idea that works extremely well in today's market. I call this my *Filthy Riches* strategy. If you would like to learn more about this, please visit **www.HUDHomesHalfOff.com** and enter access code HUD1 where you can watch a FREE 7-part Video Series, register for a training webinar, and much more.

Preparing For Closing

The next step is to begin preparing for closing. You have a fixed time frame to get your financing lined up and get ready for closing.

Some states use attorneys to close real estate transactions and some use title companies. HUD has their own attorney or title company they use in each area. In North and South Carolina they use attorneys. They have their own that they use to close all of their transactions for HUD purchases. The attorney or title company will perform a title search to make sure the property has a clean title with no liens or judgments and that HUD can transfer the deed to you free and clear.

As the buyer, you'll usually have the right to choose an attorney or title company of your choice. Two title companies can be involved—one representing the seller (HUD) and one representing the buyer (you)—if that is your choice.

If you are wholesaling the property, you will want to choose a title company of your own that understands how simultaneous closings work. Most companies don't because it's a lesser-known means of doing business, and you don't have time to educate them or try to get title insurance if their underwriters need to get educated or will not insure these kinds of deals.

In most cities, there is a real estate investors' association, where you can ask around and find out which companies in town "get it" regarding wholesaling and other kinds of creative investing. You can also ask Realtors and other investors as well.

Always get title insurance on your purchase whether it is a HUD home or other type of property purchase. When you get title insurance, you are insuring that the title to the property is free and clear of any liens and that if anything arises in the future to question your ownership then the title insurance company will defend you. It is not very expensive, and I never purchase a property without it. The attorney or title company handling the closing will take care of this for you.

Usually the day before closing, you will receive a HUD1 closing statement, which will detail the entire transaction and include all closing costs and who is paying them. This HUD1 closing statement will tell you exactly how much money you have to bring to closing and how much the seller (HUD in this case) will net at closing.

You (or your partner/private lender, etc.) will send the funds to the attorney or title company to hold in their escrow account. When the day of closing comes, you will come to the title company or attorney's office and sign your loan documents, if any, settlement statement, and other disclosures and paperwork required to transfer ownership of the property from HUD to you.

After the closing, she's all yours! Follow through with your exit strategy of wholesaling, fix and flip or leasing the house for long term cash flow.

If you are wholesaling the property, you will have a second closing after this one. In this second closing, the investor buyer you found will show up and sign an additional set of paperwork for you to sell the house to them. The attorney or title company will also handle this for you.

We are actually closing so many HUD homes now that we now have a HUD attorney come to our office once a week to close deals for us. This is something that the attorney offered since he was closing so many deals for us every week. We even offered to let them use our conference room as a satellite office for other closings they need to do in our area.

Another HUD attorney in North Carolina told us that we were buying more HUD properties in North Carolina than any other single buyer he knew of. I knew we were buying a lot of HUD homes, but I didn't know that we were the largest buyers of HUD homes in North Carolina until he told us.

As I am writing this right now, we are closing about 20-25 homes a month and have 41 homes under contract. This is more properties than I have ever done. This is great, but the market we are experiencing right now will not last forever, so get out there and make some offers and you will get some deals and make some money.

Special Bonus

Short-term capital gains taxes on homes bought and sold within a year's time are higher than if you bought and held for at least a year first. Avoid paying more in taxes by investing in real estate using a IRA or other retirement account. I have a special report and audio explaining exactly how to do this. Simply go to **www.HUDHomesHalfOff.com** and enter access code HUD1.

Larry Goins

CHAPTER NINE:
Conclusion

Hopefully, by now you've seen how HUD homes can be a fantastic source of investment properties. Is it any wonder why I love them so much?

I hope you have enjoyed *HUD Homes Half Off*. I have tried to give you the most up-to-date information on HUD's website and how to navigate it, as well as how to make money on HUD homes or just find a bargain property to live in for you and your family.

I have thousands of successful students all over the United States and in other countries as well. To see and hear from them yourself please visit **www.HUDHomesHalfOff.com** where you can watch hundreds of video testimonials and read written testimonials as well. I would love to hear from you, too, when you make your first HUD purchase.

If you have any questions please do not hesitate to contact my office, as my goal in writing this book is to help you get started in buying your own HUD home for either an investment or to live in.

I also have a vested interest in helping you to become successful. I would like to fund some of your HUD home purchases or maybe buy a house from you or maybe you will even buy a house from me.

The rest is up to you! Will this be the year you take your financial situation to the next level? I have done my best to pave the way, but your passion, commitment, and work ethic are up to you. I wholeheartedly encourage you to start looking for properties and make an offer today. Don't delay!

This book is all about making money or saving money buying HUD homes. We talk a lot about money and that is why you are reading this book, but I want you to remember that money is just a tool. It is a tool that gives you the freedom to spend your time the way you want to. Money can buy you a house, but not a home. It can buy you a Rolex, but can't give you one more second of time on earth with your family. Money can pay your medical bills, but can't give you good health. And the most important thing is, money can buy you a cross to hang around your neck, but it can't give you salvation. So think about this and remember, it's not all about the money.

Many investors have found that their performance increases (or even doubles and triples) when they have a coach or mentor to hold them accountable and help them speed up the process. I actually have students that come to my office to see my whole operation and learn exactly how we buy and sell so many houses every month. We call this our Inner Circle Apprentice Program. Coming to my office is just one part of my Inner Circle Apprentice program. Be sure to ask my team member about it when you have your one-on-one strategy session, which is a bonus included with this book.

Please do not forget to take advantage of all of the other bonuses I have offered you as an owner of this book. There are many bonuses that will help you to get started right away. I will list them all here again.

$568 bonuses Include:

FREE access to my exclusive web-based Ultimate Property Analyzer software that will enable you to analyze any deal in two seconds flat! Includes a video tutorial to show you exactly how to use it!

FREE audio training and special report on how to buy real estate in your IRA or retirement account!

FREE training video of one of my Realtors making HUD offers for me live!

FREE training video on how to buy and sell your HUD homes the same day (Real Estate Day Trading!).

FREE 7 part video series on how to sell your low priced HUD homes for 3-6 times what you paid for them earning 119% returns or more by using seller financing!

FREE 30-minute strategy session call with one of my team members in my office to answer your all of your questions and to help you get started making money on HUD homes right away! During this 30 minute session, we can help you determine the best way to get started investing in real estate—whether through HUD homes specifically or through any number of the methods I practice and teach!

FREE tickets for you and a guest to my Three Day Training Boot Camp event taught personally by my team and I. We hold 6-8 of these a year all over the USA!

(continued on following page)

FREE addition to my wholesale buyers' list to get first notification of my deep discounted properties before other investors and a video presentation I have prepared for you.

FREE customized spreadsheet that I use to keep track of all of my HUD offers.

To access all of these bonuses and more just go to **www.HUDHomesHalfOff.com** and enter this access code: HUD1

Sincerely,

Larry Goins

Real Estate Investor, Author & Mentor

www.HUDHomesHalfOff.com

INDEX